SUCCESS WITH
SHADE-LOVING PLANTS

SUCCESS WITH

SHADE-LOVING PLANTS

Graham Clarke

GUILD OF MASTER CRAFTSMAN
PUBLICATIONS LTD

First published 2007 by
Guild of Master Craftsman Publications Ltd
Castle Place, 166 High Street,
Lewes, East Sussex BN7 1XU

All of the pictures were taken by the author, except for those listed below:
Front cover: GAP Photos/John Glover
GMC/Eric Sawford: Back cover, from top, first and third down, pages 77
(left), 78 (top), 83 (both), 84, 86, 88, 89, 90, 91, 92, 95 (both), 96,
97 (both), 98 (both), 99, 100, 101 (both), 102, 103 (both), 104, 105
(both), 107, 108, 109 (both), 110, 111 (both), 112, 113 (both), 114,
115 (both), 116, 117 (both), 124, 125 (both), 126, 127 (bottom), 133
(top), 137 (bottom), 138, 139 (top), 140, 141, 143 (top), 145 (both),
147, 149 (bottom), 151 (both).
Hozelock: 41, 59, 63 (left). Etesia: 48 (left).
Dobies Seeds: 153 (bottom). Suttons Seeds: 155.

ISBN: 978-1-86108-469-9

A catalogue record for this book is available from the British Library.

Managing Editor: Gerrie Purcell
Production Manager: Jim Bulley
Editor: Virginia Brehaut
Managing Art Editor: Gilda Pacitti
Designer: John Hawkins

Set in Futura

Colour origination by Altaimage
Printed and bound by Sino Publishing

Contents

LEFT It is usually recommended that ponds are placed in sunny spots, but small water features such as this perpetually filling sink feature can be sited in dark corners of the garden.

ABOVE **Placing a seat in a shady spot can make a welcome respite from intense summer heat.**

Introduction

As a trained gardener who lives in the UK, I am conditioned when buying a house to look first and foremost at whether the back garden is south-facing. Actually, if it faces any direction other than south, then the house has to work very hard indeed to capture my imagination. For a south-facing garden in the UK (and anywhere in the northern hemisphere) means that it is pointing the best way to receive the greatest amounts of precious sunlight. It means that the garden will be light, and we are able to grow the widest variety of plants. If you live in the southern hemisphere the sunniest direction is northwards.

If you think about it, there are probably around three times more gardens, across the planet, that do not face the sun directly. They may be west- or east-facing, or even facing completely away from the sun so that for the main part of the day it is behind you rather than in front. For all of these gardens you can guarantee that there will be fairly dense areas of shade at certain times, and that means you should be aware of the plants that are either happiest in such places, or at least are tolerant of them.

Shade in the garden is often considered to be a problem, some think nothing will grow except perhaps a green carpet of moss (actually, this can be a rather attractive feature in the dense shade of a large tree). In fact, shade should be regarded as an asset rather than a problem, for it enables one to grow an even wider range of plants than would be possible in a garden completely bathed in sunshine.

To make things more complex, there are varying degrees of shade – from 'deep' at one extreme to 'dappled' at the other. There are different plants suited to different degrees of shade. There are true shade-lovers (generally those plants that grow under trees in their natural habitats), and then there are those plants that are very adaptable, growing and flowering equally well in sun or shade. Experimenting with plants is very important: if a particular plant appeals and you are unsure of the conditions it requires, then try it in shade. If it begins to look poorly, move it to a sunnier spot. Gardening is a very fluid activity.

You should also bear in mind that there is an equally wide range of plants that will not tolerate shade – these are the sun-lovers. These come from warm or hot, often dry, places in the wild. The sun-lovers need really bright light and plenty of direct sun. Although they may survive in shade they will not grow and flower well.

Before we get in to the book proper, I want to dispel the myth that shady gardens are dark and dull. This may be the case in some instances, but the reason for this is that the gardeners have chosen the wrong plants. I love a gardening challenge, and a garden with plenty of shade certainly offers this. If you find yourself with such a garden, I hope you'll get plenty of rewarding ideas from this book.

AWARD OF GARDEN MERIT

Throughout this book you will see the initials AGM set after certain plants. This denotes that the plant in question has passed certain assessments carried out by experts under the auspices of the Royal Horticultural Society in Great Britain. Only plants with exceptionally good garden qualities can be awarded this special Award of Garden Merit.

LEFT **If you have the space, why not create a 'woodland'
garden; enabling you to grow a range of shade-loving
plants in what otherwise may be a sunny area.**

CHAPTER 1

What is shade, and what does it do?

It may seem a strange point, but have you ever really thought about shade. What is it? In the simplest of terms it is an area that does not receive direct sunlight, owing to some obstruction or blockage preventing the sun's rays from directly falling on to it. But it is not as simple as that. There are varying degrees of shade, and they can be effectively broken down into four categories: deep, light, dappled and partial.

ABOVE Deep shade is where light intensity is very low, such as under large trees as well as between tall buildings and in basement gardens.

DEEP SHADE

This is where the light intensity is very low, and the area is quite dark and gloomy. Such conditions are found under large trees with dense foliage, particularly evergreens and conifers, as well as between large buildings, and basement gardens. As if the light level problem was not bad enough, the soil in such places is usually very dry for much of the time. The soil at the base of walls is dry because the structure above deflects rainfall, and the roots of trees – especially large ones – extract huge amounts of moisture from the ground.

If it was simply just a case of heavy shade, or of a dry soil, then we could find many types of suitable plant. But it is the combination of shade and dryness that creates the challenge. There are relatively few plants that can thrive in this kind of situation, but of those that do, the ivies (forms of *Hedera*), St John's wort (*Hypericum*) and butcher's broom (*Ruscus*) are perhaps the most familiar.

ABOVE Light shade is the shade cast by walls, hedges and so on, but where the area is also open to the sky, so there is still some brightness.

LIGHT SHADE

This is the shade cast by walls, buildings, hedges and so on, but with the area open to the sky. Therefore there may be little or no sun, but still the light is bright. The soil can also be dry in this situation, particularly immediately in front of a wall. Many attractive plants can be grown here, and particularly climbing plants (including a few roses, which normally are sun-lovers). Low-growing plants suited to these conditions include ferns and most forms of *Hosta*.

DAPPLED SHADE

The area in question here will have sunlight filtering through when the sun is in a certain direction. Many trees, particularly deciduous kinds that drop their leaves in the autumn, provide the most useful form of shade. Their light foliage canopies allow through some of the sun's rays, but as the sun moves across the sky, so different areas are illuminated.

Not surprisingly, it is woodland plants that are most suited to dappled shade. These are often some of the most attractive of garden plants,

ABOVE Dappled shade is where sunlight is filtered through trees and tall shrubs, and it is the usual type of light found in woodlands.

and they include the many forms of *Primula*, as well as snowdrops, bluebells, and the wonderful blue poppy (*Meconopsis*). In addition to dappled shade, most of these plants also grow best in soil that remains moist for most of the time. This is most often found in light woodland, where the trees are well spaced.

13

PARTIAL SHADE

This is an area of the garden that is shaded for part of the day, but also receives full sun at times as well. The area may, for example, be shaded by buildings in the morning, but is sunny for the rest of the day. This kind of shade does not fall within the scope of this book as the areas concerned receive an average amount of sunlight, enabling a very wide range of plants to be grown, which includes those that we call the 'sun-loving plants'.

WHAT DOES SHADE DO?

In order to understand the importance of shade – for it is not necessarily a 'problem', but actually an 'asset', we should first have a short botany lesson. All plants, both shade and sun-tolerant, are essentially green. Those with yellow or variegated leaves have large areas of green on them, and those with purple leaves are actually green underneath.

The green colouring in plants is due to the presence of a chemical pigment called chlorophyll, which is sometimes masked by pigments of other colours. It is not present in animals, nor in fungi, but occurs in algae, all

flowering plants and ferns. I would even go as far as to say that, as a chemical, it ranks as one of, if not the most important chemicals on Earth.

Those plants that contain it have an ability to use sunlight to manufacture essential food from the raw materials of carbon dioxide and water, in a process called photosynthesis. In a shady garden sunlight is, or can be, in short supply. Therefore the plants that have evolved, or been bred, to be tolerant of shade, do not need as much direct sunlight in order to function properly.

Some ferns have developed a tolerance of some of the lowest light levels, and many are seen growing naturally in gloomy places such as caves and on the internal walls of deep wells. It follows, therefore, that if a plant has leaves that are deficient in chlorophyll (such as variegated plants, where the chlorophyll is confined to certain areas), it will have a problem growing in a low-light area. This manifests itself in the plants being less vigorous, and possibly stunted, and very much 'poor relations' to their all-green counterparts. In fact, some variegated plants if grown in a shady place will readily revert to being an all green plant and, depending on several factors, this could happen within one

ABOVE Variegated leaves, such as with this holly (*Ilex x altaclerensis* 'Golden King'), have large areas of green on them, needing sunlight to bring out the best colourings.

ABOVE Some ferns have evolved to tolerate some of the lowest light levels, and many actually thrive in the gloomiest of places.

ABOVE Plants with yellow, reddish or purple leaves (such as this *Phormium* 'Platt's Black'), seem to have less of a problem growing in shade.

ABOVE Many shade-loving plants, including hostas (this is *Hosta tokudama flavocircinalis*), have large, flattened leaves, designed to receive as much light as is available.

growing season. Plants with reddish, purple or yellow leaves seem to have less of a problem with shade, because the chlorophyll is not absent or lacking, it is just masked to our eyes by another pigment.

THE ISSUE OF MOISTURE LOSS

Generally, plants that have adapted to shady conditions have relatively large, flattened leaves, and often set at angles designed to receive as much light across their surface as possible: think of forms of *Hosta*, *Fatsia*, *Rodgersia* or even *Gunnera* with its leaves often 10ft (3m) across. If you looked at these leaves under the microscope you would be able to see that they all have very thin surface cell layers, to facilitate better penetration of light to the cells that contain chlorophyll.

But leaves also transpire – losing water to the atmosphere (to be replaced by moisture drawn up the plant via its roots). The large, flat leaves that are designed to receive sunlight also have the largest area from which to transpire moisture,

which can lead to dehydration and death. Fortunately, however, most shady plants also prefer reasonably damp soils, and this not only provides a constant source of moisture for the roots to take up, but there is inevitably a humid localized atmosphere around the plants, which helps to reduce evaporation from the leaves.

The real problem occurs in those parts of a garden that are both shady and dry. The leaves, and in fact the whole plant, need to work extra hard to capture sufficient moisture to grow satisfactorily, and sufficient sunlight to provide itself with energy. It means that the ivies, St John's wort and butcher's brooms should not be thought of as dull and uninteresting, but hard-working, beleaguered plants that should be treasured.

ABOVE Ivies are one of the few plants that thrive in conditions that are both dry and shady.

CHAPTER 2

Designing your garden to make the most of shade

If your garden receives large amounts of shade, be it heavy, light or dappled, the only way to counter it is to reduce the size(s) of the objects causing the shade. If the main shade comes from tall or large buildings, well, sadly you are not going to be able to do anything, short of organized demolition. If, on the other hand, the shade in your garden is created by woody plant material then the situation is much more manageable.

ABOVE Trees filter the light reaching the ground, but if they cast too much shade, you can thin them out.

THINNING OUT TREES AND SHRUBS

In the case of trees, they can perhaps be thinned out. A dense jungle of a garden, maybe one that has been neglected and allowed to over-grow, will probably have shrubs and even trees growing into each other, with the branches intertwining. This will create very dark conditions below, especially when the trees are in leaf, and in these situations you may often expect to find pernicious plants such as brambles or bracken thriving healthily.

You need to carry out some drastic but systematic pruning here. If you need to get high into a tree to thin out its branches, this is probably best carried out by a professional tree surgeon who will have the correct equipment, expertise and, dare I say, insurance! Trees may be protected by a Tree Preservation Order, which will prevent you from felling or making significant alterations to them; if you are not sure about this, a quick call to the appropriate department at your local authority, where such trees are registered, will give you an answer.

You may be able to thin out lower branches and shrubs yourself. The best time to do this is during the dormant period from late autumn to late winter. This is when you will cause least damage to plants' growth buds. However, my view is that if your garden is densely shady, and you are able to rectify this by thinning out plant growth, you should get it done as soon as possible – whichever time of year that may be.

After thinning out, what then happens can be amazing. Wild foxgloves (*Digitalis*) may spring up from, seemingly, nowhere! Plant growth – in the main of course, weeds and wild plants, the seeds of which have lain dormant in the soil – will quickly colonize the area now that it is receiving light and the sun's warmth, and it has a good air circulation.

To convert these areas so they become useful, decorative beds and borders you will need to exercise a weeding regime, and then condition the soil so it is ready for planting.

ABOVE **Thick trees that have matted together, in this case an apple and a magnolia, can create dense shade when in full leaf.**

ABOVE **When major work on trees is required, it is always better to employ the services of a professional tree surgeon.**

ABOVE **When tree canopies open up there is suddenly light and air, and plants such as foxgloves (*Digitalis*) are commonly found – as if appearing from nowhere.**

HEDGES

Hedges are a mixed blessing. On the one hand they give us privacy and seclusion, and they help to keep out undesirables. But on the other hand, they also cast shade and take away much of the moisture from the soil. Any hedge should be maintained regularly. This may involve a simple reduction of over-long stems (in the case of an informal or flowering hedge), or it may be a far more involved, twice-yearly clipping using ladders, straight lines to give an edge, and an array of cutting paraphernalia, from simple shears to complex powered hedge trimmers.

If you are in possession of a tall or overgrown hedge, it will most certainly be causing more shade than you would ideally like, and the only two options to resolve this are to cut back the hedge to a desirable height and width, or to remove it completely – roots and all.

The latter sounds drastic but this is exactly what I have done in my garden. When we moved here we inherited a large overgrown hedge of the notorious fast-growing Leyland cypress (x *Cupressocyparis leylandii*). It had reached a height of 40ft (12m). It was growing at the bottom of a south-facing garden, which for us meant a very shady lawn for much of the day.

We knew we could not live with this, so soon after moving in we had the top half of the conifers removed. This allowed a considerable amount of light into the garden. It created quite an ugly hedge with masses of bare wood showing, but we decided to live with this for the best part of a year, for two reasons. First, to see if the bare, exposed branches would re-grow and become clothed in new, green shoots, and second, to see if the new height of the hedge

REMOVING A HEDGE TO LET IN

1 An old, overgrown hedge in the author's garden cast too much shade on to the lawn, and rendered much of the garden unworkable. Nothing would grow near it.

2 It was decided to have the hedge removed; the first things to cut back were the side branches, which then exposed the sizeable trunks.

3 The 'trees' which made up the hedge were too large to be pulled out, so they were cut at ground level; they were applied with brushwood killer to hasten their rotting.

would allow us to grow a greater variety of plants, and enable the lawn to become less mossy; moss growth is a prime symptom of a lawn that is too shady.

Well, the branches did not re-grow, and the bare wood remained bare, and quite an eyesore. Also, the act of reducing the height of the hedge simply gave us the appetite to go the whole way. So, last winter we removed the offending stretch of hedge completely. This has resulted in a stronger, healthier lawn, and we have been able to create a new mixed border with small shrubs, perennials, bulbs and summer flowers, and it has transformed the whole of the garden.

RIGHT **Hedges can cast heavy shade, so they should be trimmed regularly, and at least twice a year if you are growing the fast-growing Leyland cypress (x *Cupressocyparis leylandii*).**

4 The rotting stumps were covered with plastic to prevent them drying out; trellis panels were fixed to the boundary walls, and a bed was marked out.

5 Variegated ivies were planted against the trelliswork and mixed plants were chosen to fill the new bed; some require shade (that is cast by the wall).

DESIGN TRICKS TO REDUCE THE IMPACT OF SHADE

CONTAINERS

Perhaps the best, and certainly the simplest way to introduce colour and interest into a shaded part of the garden is to use plants in containers such as pots, tubs, urns, vases, troughs, hanging baskets and windowboxes. The advantages to this are that the plants will grow in prepared compost, so the condition of the garden soil is not relevant; the plants are easily fed and watered; and they can be moved around the garden at will. Any plants that are past their best can be moved from sight and replaced with others. Remember that plants needing plenty of sunlight do not mind having short periods in the shade, so these can be used to really brighten up a dull area.

CONSTRUCTION MATERIALS

In a shady garden one should try to use light-coloured materials for walls, patio paving, containers and so on. They will brighten an area by reflecting light. Huge ranges of pre-cast paving and walling stone, and bright containers, are available from garden centres and DIY stores, and your main problem is likely to be in making the choice.

Pea shingle (fingernail-sized stones or gravel) usually comes in shades of light brown or cream, and other stone is available in bright, or even prime colours. Using this sort of material for pathways, or as a covering on beds or the soil in containers, can add brightness or real colour to a shaded garden.

ABOVE Containers with colourful plants can be moved to shady parts of the garden to brighten them up, and then moved back when the flowering has finished.

ABOVE **Light paving and patio materials, as seen in the patio under construction, help to brighten a darkly shaded area.**

ABOVE **Modern garden designers favour contemporary mulching materials, such as coloured glass chippings, but they do not suit every garden.**

Walls are usually built of brick, block walling or breeze block, but there is also screen block walling. Made from concrete, these have open, patterned shapes that let in a fair amount of light. Using this material can alter an area of dense shade to one of dappled shade. Screen blocks became extremely popular in garden schemes during the 1970s, and in recent years have been considered a little old-fashioned. However, they can be used to great effect in a shaded garden, and I would much prefer to be a successful, old-fashioned gardener than a failed gardener because of lack of light!

The ubiquitous larch-lap fencing in panels serves a purpose, but is dreadfully boring and creates high levels of shade. You may not really have much option to change this if the fence is not yours, but belongs to a neighbour, or you wish to have something solid for the sake of privacy. However, there are instances when replacing these solid affairs with more open or light alternatives can again change the status of a garden from 'dense shade' to 'dappled'.

Timber, ranch-style fencing is often used and can be very attractive in some settings. Similarly picket fencing, if painted white, can be very appealing, and is most appropriate on an older-style property with a cottage-style garden. To divide a garden internally, rather than using panel fencing, use panel trellis screens, possibly painted white.

RAISED BEDS

The area under trees, as we have already seen, can be shaded and dry. The other disadvantage is that you are unlikely to get much of a depth of soil before you come to a mass of tangled tree roots. One way to resolve this is to create a

ABOVE **Raised beds, especially against a wall with foundations or under trees, can enable you to raise plants so that there is a better depth of soil in which to grow them.**

raised bed. Here, the soil level is lifted significantly above all the existing troublesome roots and dusty, compacted earth. Be warned, however: raised beds under trees are fine, but do not be tempted to raise the soil level so that it comes further up a tree's trunk, as this will kill it. Instead, raise the soil at the front of the bed, but then gradually reduce the level as you approach the tree.

Even raising a bed by a mere 12in (30cm) will provide enough additional depth for many perennials and small shrubs. Large growing plants will need greater soil depth. You will need to put in place some retaining walls to prevent the soil from falling or washing away. You can use brick blocks for this, but a simpler solution would be to place some old railway sleepers down, and infill these with fresh soil. You can stack them for greater height. They are widely

available; look for suppliers in the *Yellow Pages*. Do not use plastic edging materials, or log rolls, as these can give an artificial look, and are probably too flimsy to do the job properly.

Raised beds also allow you to grow a wider range of plants. For example, if your soil is mainly chalky, you can create a bed for acid-loving plants, such as heathers, rhododendrons and camellias, by filling it with acid soil, as well as quantities of peat, and dressing the area annually with ericaceous fertilizers (which are formulated for acid-loving plants).

EXTERIOR DECORATING

Dark, gloomy corners can be as a result of high walls preventing the access of light: just think of basement gardens in towns and cities. These dark areas can often be improved by painting the walls a light colour, using cream, white or any other light pastel-coloured masonry paint. Dark (or 'saturated') colours absorb light and make an area like this seem much gloomier.

You could also consider mounting a large mirror on one (or more) of the walls. This will not only reflect light but will also create the illusion of depth, by reflecting a part of the garden. This can be very useful with a small garden: a mirror can make it look much bigger than it really is. The idea of using garden mirrors is not new, but it has gained in popularity over the past few years. Framing the mirror will help the illusion, rather than making it look simply like a mirror hung on a garden wall! False-perspective trellis units, where the wooden slats are not at right angles, are available with mirrors backing them. This can even give the impression of an arched pathway. If you site the mirror directly at the end of a pathway, and then frame it with a false door frame, you will give the illusion of a secret garden the other side of the wall. All of these ideas are a bit of fun, but do make sure that the mirror you use is toughened, and suitable for outdoor use. Indoor mirrors may shatter in extremely cold winter weather.

ABOVE **Areas of a garden that are dark and gloomy can be brightened up with colourful walls and the use of mirrors, as seen in this contemporary design.**

ABOVE **Garden ornaments, such as this sandstone-coloured wild boar, can really provide a focal point in an otherwise dark garden.**

ORNAMENTS

Garden ornaments and statuary can add the finishing touch to a garden setting, and they certainly give it character. As with paving and walling materials, light-coloured ornaments are recommended for shady areas as they show up better than items in, say, bronze or iron.

As with the containers into which you can set plants, there is a huge range of bright and light ornaments available, and a trip to a local garden centre should give plenty of ideas. But do not overdo it with statuary. Rather than have six or seven items all vying for attention, one or two strategically placed items can be much more visually effective.

The idea is to create a focal point with these items, and the best way to do this is to site them, say, at the end of a path, wherever a path changes direction, in a corner of the garden or at the end of the lawn.

ABOVE **Classic garden statuary can help to take the eye away from dark recesses or corners, where the plants may be less interesting.**

23

USING THE SHADE FOR THINGS OTHER THAN PLANTS

If you have some shaded areas and you do not want to go to the trouble of, or it is impossible to change it to allow in more light, then you will have to resort to using the space for things other than plants. A water butt or tank, for example, is perfectly placed in such a shaded area. It is not desirable for the water inside to be in the full glare of the sun as, when it heats up, bacteria can quickly form.

If space permits, a shady corner may be the ideal place for a garden shed or storage unit. A level surface and privacy from potential thieves are more important factors then whether the site is shady or sunny. Dustbins are actually better if placed in the shade, as intense sunlight, particularly in summer, can cause foodstuffs to rot and the smells emanating from them can be unpleasant in the extreme.

Cars and other vehicles do not require sunshine, so if you need to have space for a vehicle, consider putting it in the shade rather than using up a valuable sunny spot. A shady spot is not suitable, however, for greenhouses, coldframes, ponds, or washing lines, as all of these ideally need direct sunlight at least for part of the day.

SUNNY GARDENS NEED SOME SHADE

There are gardens, of course – perhaps new ones or those in very open locations – which are sunny all day long, with only small areas of partial shade cast by the house. There is not much scope in these sorts of gardens for growing a collection of shade-loving plants unless one sets out to create more shady areas. This would help you to create a cooler, more restful and romantic garden. Although most of us like the sun, the glaring effect of an un-shaded garden can be rather uncomfortable all day long, and particularly in the heat of summer. A combination of sunny and shady areas also gives a garden character. Let's look, then, at what we can do to create shade in a shade-less garden.

ABOVE **Along with dustbins and compost heaps, water butts are ideal for positioning in a shady part of the garden; in full sun all of these can get very hot, which can cause them problems.**

ABOVE **Whereas patios are best positioned where they can receive full sun, a car on a driveway does not need it and, in fact, a sunny driveway is a waste of sunlight!**

THE BENEFITS OF SHADY AREAS

- ◆ They provide a cool and relaxing place to sit on a hot day.
- ◆ They add character to a garden by creating areas with different moods.
- ◆ The varieties of plants that you can grow are widened.

TREES

Deciduous trees with a light canopy of foliage provide the best type of shade – dappled – so if space permits try planting a few trees. Even a small group will create an attractive mini woodland area, which will provide the right conditions for a host of garden plants you would not otherwise be able to grow. Trees need not be huge affairs: there are plenty to choose from for all but the smallest of gardens (see pages 134–151 for a selection of shade-loving types).

Most people plant trees as single specimens, but if you want to plant a small group for the mini-woodland effect, it is best to use just one species. A group of *Malus* (apples or crab apples), *Sorbus* (mountain ashes, rowans or whitebeams) or *Betula* (birches) could achieve the effect you desire.

In each case you will want some idea of the ultimate spread of the trees. Here we come to a difficult aspect because the spread of a tree depends upon its surroundings. For example, the branches of trees that are growing very close together, or which are surrounded by tall buildings, tend to grow upright with very little outward spread. But trees with plenty of space around them will spread more. Generally, however, you can assume that the ultimate spread of a tree will be approximately 40 per cent of the final height.

ABOVE **Lightly canopied trees, such as this snakebark maple (*Acer griseum*), can cast useful dappled shade in an otherwise sunny garden.**

ABOVE **Mature trees can cast very useful dappled shade.**

TREES TO GROW FOR SHADE

Trees that create and cast shade are many and various, but the following are some of the best for small to medium-sized garden situations, and they each have assets of their own to promote:

Ornamental cherry: There are many forms of ornamental cherry (*Prunus*), but the following are two that are fabulous when gardens are not particularly colourful. *Prunus subhirtella* 'Autumnalis' is known as the autumn or winter cherry, and it produces masses of small semi-double white flowers during mild spells throughout both of these seasons. It will reach a height of 30ft (10m) at maturity – ten years. Slightly larger is *Prunus sargentiana*. This tree is famed for its spectacular autumn colour, when its leaves change from green to vibrant shades of red and orange. Pink flowers appear amongst the unfurling young, bronzy leaves in early spring. It will eventually reach a high of 50ft (15m).

ABOVE The twisted stems of *Corylus avellana* 'Contorta' provide dappled shade, but are a good garden feature in their own right.

Mountain ash or rowan: *Sorbus aucuparia* grows wild in many parts of the UK and other temperate countries throughout Europe and North America. In spring it is shrouded with white flowers, while in the autumn it is clothed with bunches of reddish-orange berries (if the birds leave them alone). It reaches a height at maturity of 40ft (12m).

Maple: Several of the maple family (forms of *Acer*) provide the type of shade we desire. Try *Acer griseum*, one of several types commonly referred to as a 'snakebark maple'. As you might expect, its bark is decorative, being predominately green with whitish stripes. New twig growth is bright red, giving a secondary attraction in spring. It will eventually reach a height of 30ft (10m).

Twisted hazel: *Corylus avellana* 'Contorta' will reach an eventual height of 20ft (6m), and it provides lovely dappled shade. Its own attraction, however, comes from its twisted and contorted stems that are at their most visible in the winter without the leaves.

Birches: Forms of *Betula* are fine on their own, but look especially good when grown in groups of three or more. The common silver birch (*Betula pendula*) has white bark and a dainty, light canopy. It will grow to some 50ft (15m) or so, but it can be topped several times to keep the height under control. One of the main drawbacks of birch, however, is that these trees are surface-rooters, which means that the roots are just beneath the soil surface, and this makes planting under them both difficult to do, and unappealing to plants as the soil will be very dry.

BUILDINGS

In addition to the dwelling, which may or may not be casting useful amounts of shade, you could consider building other permanent structures. A summerhouse or gazebo, for example, usually has one or two solid sides; with the remaining sides being fully open to sunlight. The shaded area immediately behind a summerhouse, if there is space, can be useful for planting. The same applies to garden sheds, garages and larger storage units. A greenhouse, although made of glass and seemingly transparent, does filter sunlight and on the darker side of it there will be useful dappled shade.

ABOVE **This simple wicker-sided gazebo casts useful shade in an otherwise open garden.**

ABOVE **An open summerhouse, such as this ornate timber structure, will provide summer shade for the plants surrounding it, and the gardener as well!**

LEFT **A greenhouse, here painted white for summer to help shade the plants inside, will filter sunlight, creating dappled shade on the darker side.**

ARCHES, PERGOLAS AND ARBOURS

An archway may provide some shade, but it may be too small to be that effective. Better still, a timber pergola – which is essentially a series of two or more attached arches – could be built. 'Arbour' is the name for a sitting area, originally to be surrounded by trees. Today it usually means a sitting area with a canopy of wood above you, very often designed simply to act as a shade from the sun. Up all of these structures you can grow a range of climbing plants to hide the sharp lines, and provide dappled shade.

Pergolas are most often found on a patio and/or close to the house. This is so that one can entertain under them, and perhaps be sheltered from the heat of the summer sun. But a free-standing pergola can be placed anywhere in the garden. If it is away from the patio there needs to be a 'reason' for it in design terms, and this reason could be, for example, to walk through it to see a little statue situated at the far end, or it can be a walkway through to a vegetable or fruit-growing area.

Regardless of where and why you erect a pergola, the point here is that it provides useful shade. On a patio it could be set next to small raised beds where shade-loving plants can be grown. Alternatively, if your pergola is over a garden path you could grow plants in narrow borders on each side of the path. You can choose some fairly quick-growing climbers to grow over the pergola. These can, of course, be sun-loving plants as their tops will be in full sun.

ABOVE **This small blue-painted arbour was placed in a sunny part of the garden to provide some respite from intense summer sun.**

PLANTS TO GROW OVER PERGOLAS

Larger pergolas could accommodate a *Laburnum* which, in spring, will drip with bunches of golden flowers. This is known as a 'Laburnum arch'. Or instead you could grow a *Wisteria*, which, every spring, will drip with bunches of highly fragrant purple, lilac or white flowers.

If you are planning to sit in the shade of a pergola, the scent from the flowers growing over the structure could be important. Apart from *Wisteria* you could choose any of the honeysuckles (*Lonicera*), jasmines (*Jasminum*), or climbing roses (*Rosa*) although with these latter plants you may need to watch out for the thorns!

ABOVE **Hedges are natural providers of shade; this is the dark-leaved copper beech (*Fagus sylvatica* form *purpurea*).**

SCREENS AND HEDGES

For me, one of the most important parts of garden design, as long as space allows it, is to create a garden that cannot be seen in its entirety from the house. To create an element of surprise a garden should, if possible, be divided into several smaller areas. These divisions can be made with hedges, either formal (with straight sides) or informal (comprising shrubs – often flowering types – but invariably with arching stems billowing into each other). Walls and fences take up less space; you could choose from bricks or screen blocks; or you could use panel fencing or trelliswork.

Hedges and screens will have a shady side if they are suitably positioned, and this will certainly help to create a better garden. In the northern hemisphere the shady side will be north facing, and in the southern hemisphere this will be south facing. Climbing plants can be grown up screens formed of timber trellis panels or screen-block walling.

DESIGN CONCLUSION

Large shrubs and small trees planted anywhere in a garden will all help to provide shady areas, but the rule is not to overdo it. If you crowd too many of these into a space you will merely create a gloomy garden. Aim to achieve a balance between sunny and shady areas, and then you will be able to grow the widest variety of plants possible.

CHAPTER 3

Buying and planting shade-loving plants

Once you have decided which shade-loving plants to grow (see section two of this book for the descriptions of suitable plants), and you have decided where you want to grow them, you will need to buy and plant them. The choice of plants is,

frankly, enormous, and the different ways to buy and set them out can bewilder a beginner to gardening – and sometimes the more experienced of us as well. Let's look at the different plant groups, how to buy them, and get them planted.

ANNUALS, BIENNIALS AND BEDDING PLANTS

Annuals are plants that are sown, grow, flower and die all within a year, whereas biennials are sown and grown on in one year, and flower and die during a second year. Bedding plants is the term used to describe plants of either type, generally grown in quantity, and planted in 'beds', for a massed display. These include the fibrous-rooted bedding begonia (*Begonia semperflorens*), sweet Williams (*Dianthus barbatus*), foxgloves (*Digitalis purpureus*) and polyanthus (hybrids of *Primula x polyantha*).

Bedding plants are usually sold in trays or pots and, depending on the type, are available from six months before they are due to flower, right up until they have already started to flower. When choosing them from a garden centre or shop, look for healthy specimens. There should be no weeds, or pests or diseases present. And the ideal plant will not yet have started to flower, which will mean that you have a full season of colour ahead of you. If they have already started blooming the plants will have developed a

ABOVE **Buying plants that are suitable for a shady garden is not a straightforward process – each label will need to be read to check that the plant is appropriate.**

ABOVE Spring bedding for shade, such as primulas (including these polyanthus varieties), are generally sold in packs of six or twelve.

ABOVE Violas and pansies, which perform very well in light shade, are sold by the million, and these are available for flowering almost throughout the year.

significant root system and may respond badly when planted out. You will also have missed some of the flowering potential. If the plants you desire have all started to flower whilst still on the shop's shelves, the aim should be to go for the trays, or plants, with the fewest flowers.

Whether you have sown your own bedding plants from seed, or bought your plants from a garden centre, they will eventually need planting out. Most annual types will be tender (in that they will be damaged by frost or very cold weather). So these plants, which will have been started into growth in a greenhouse, will need very slow acclimatization in spring to colder conditions – a term known as 'hardening off'. They should not, of course, be fully planted out in the garden or in containers until all danger of frosts has passed.

The soil in which they are to grow should be as well prepared as possible, as this can affect the performance of the plants during their short

lives most directly. Before planting, fork the soil over, making sure that any annual weeds are completely buried. Perennial weeds however should be removed as these will re-grow if left. To feed the bedding plants through the season, apply a sprinkling of general fertilizer evenly over the soil making sure you follow the manufacturer's instructions.

An hour or two before planting, give the plants a thorough watering. If the bedding plants are in individual pots, gently remove them and place them in a hole dug with a trowel. The hole should be the same size as the pot. Firm them in place with your hands and water them in.

If the plants are in plastic or polystyrene strips, you will need to either break the strips apart, or gently tease the plants out of their compartments. In each case, try to do as little damage to the roots and stems as possible. Damaged leaves will readily be replaced with new leaves, within reason, but a plant only has one stem!

BULBS

Mention garden bulbs to most people and they will think of the spring-flowering types, such as daffodils (*Narcissus*), tulips, crocuses, hyacinths and so on. The earlier types that flower in winter and into early spring include snowdrops (*Galanthus*) and winter aconites (*Eranthis*). In summer there are lilies, gladiolus and dahlias, while in the autumn there are colchicums, schizostylis and sternbergias. You could, in fact, create a year-round bulb garden, and it would be quite beautiful.

As for buying bulbs, mid-summer is when the first of the new season's mail order bulb catalogues drop through the letterbox. Although the following spring may seem, and is, a long way off, ordering early has many advantages: those that require early planting, such as colchicums and daffodils, will be with you in good time; also, if you delay ordering, some

varieties may be sold out later in the season. The range of bulbs available by mail order is extensive and includes unusual varieties.

Mail ordered bulbs will be selected at the nursery, so in terms of bulb quality, you are stuck with what you are sent – but do not be afraid to complain or send the bulbs back if they turn out to be substandard. Bulbs will also be on display at garden centres from mid-summer onwards, offering the opportunity to browse, choose and plan your display. Much useful information about colour, height and growing is to be found on accompanying point of sale material.

Store bulbs in a cool dry place, never near heaters – and never in plastic bags as this makes them sweat. Open any bags before planting to let air circulate. Daffodils are frequently offered for naturalizing (planting out to look like a 'natural' drift of colour, usually in a

ABOVE **A hand-held bulb planter removes a plug of soil when pushed into the ground**

ABOVE Daffodils are frequently sold for naturalizing, where they are needed in quantity, so they usually come in large netted bags.

SELECTING BULBS FROM A SHOP

There are a number of important points to remember when selecting bulbs from a shop or garden centre:

Avoid bulbs that:
◆ do not have a clean base
◆ are soft or showing signs of rot
◆ are dried out
◆ have started to shoot, producing more than a very small amount of growth

Choose bulbs that:
◆ are plump and well rounded
◆ are fleshy and firm
◆ larger bulbs usually result in the finest flower spikes

ABOVE **Clean up bulbs, removing any soil or loose skins, before storing them. Keep them in a cool, dry place, never near to heaters, and never in plastic bags as they will sweat.**

grassed area), and these are often sold in large bags. These will contain a mixture of varieties and at a competitive price. Alternatively, you can usually make your own selection of bulbs from large bins.

Plant out the bulbs out as soon as possible, labelling the place to avoid any accidental damage. Textbooks often quote very specific depths for bulbs when they are planted. As a general rule, however, a bulb should be planted so that there is as much soil above it as the height of the bulb itself; you won't go far wrong with this. Exceptions are bluebells and daffodils, which should be planted twice their own depth.

The spring-flowering bulbs are the first to be planted during the 'bulb year' and these should go in during the autumn. Daffodils and other forms of *Narcissus* could be planted in late summer or beginning of autumn, as they produce roots early. The majority of bulbs, with the exception of tulips, can be planted as soon as the summer bedding has been removed or when the ground is vacant. In the case of tulips they should be planted from mid-autumn onwards; too early, and any emerging new growth may be damaged by frost. Summer-flowering bulbs, such as gladioli and dahlias, are planted in the spring. These two, and many other types of summer bulb, are tender and will need lifting or otherwise protecting in the winter. Lilies can be set out in the autumn.

Most gardeners prefer to use a trowel. There are special graduated bulb planting trowels available; these have a long narrow blade with measurements marked on, making it easier to determine the correct depth. Always ensure the base of the bulb is in contact with the ground. Air pockets result in the roots failing to develop.

Unless you are planning formal beds, plant in groups; this is much more effective. If you are planting bulbs in grass a hand-held bulb planter is helpful, this removes a plug of soil when pushed into the ground. The bulb is inserted and the plug replaced; it is a much quicker method when large numbers are involved. Some people may be allergic to handling daffodils, tulips and hyacinth bulbs; they can cause a rash on the skin. If in doubt, use gloves.

PERENNIALS, ALPINES, FERNS AND ORNAMENTAL GRASSES

These are all plants that, although not woody, will survive and provide you with colour and interest from year to year. In most cases after four or five years it would be recommended that you lift the plants out of the ground and split, or divide them, and then to replant them. This not only stops the plant from getting too large and cumbersome, but also gives it a new lease of life (for you would only replant the healthiest and most vigorous portions). Division in this way also is a form of propagation, so from one 'mother' plant you could end up with anything from two to twenty plants, depending on what it is and how big it has become.

All of the plants in this group are generally grown in pots at the nursery, and this is how you buy them. Buy the best plants you can find. Look for vigorous, healthy specimens; they should also be young, as these will tend to establish and grow away quickly. You should not, however, buy the largest plants you see necessarily: these may be pot bound and will take time to establish. If you do end up buying a perennial plant that is pot bound, at planting time gently tease out as many of the roots from the congested 'ball' of root as possible, but try not to damage them too much.

Ideally, perennials should be planted in the spring or autumn; early-flowering subjects (such as forms of *Helleborus* and *Bergenia*) are best planted in the autumn so that they have a chance to settle in before flowering. Water the plants in their pots thoroughly an hour or two before planting them. This is so that the plant has

ABOVE **Ferns have evolved into shade-loving plants, as seen here in this man-made grotto.**

plenty of moisture in its system in advance of the 'shock' of having its roots exposed to the air and possibly become damaged – even if this is just for a mere matter of seconds. This is especially important during hot, dry spells, or windy weather conditions.

When planting a brand new border it is a good idea to set out the plants whilst they are still in their pots. This will give you an idea of what the eventual display will look like (although you will need a little imagination to visualize what they'll look like when fully grown). You can then improve the spacings and placings accordingly. Most plant labels that come with your purchases give dimensions of height and spread when the plants are fully grown, and it is important to take note of these. It is all too easy to plant perennials too close to each other. This can cause problems when they grow; it can encourage weak and spindly growth, and make the plants more susceptible to attack by fungal diseases.

For each plant dig a hole that is large enough to accommodate the entire root system. Depending on the size of the plant this may require the use of a trowel or a spade. Carefully remove the plant from its container and, if possible, spread out the roots as you place the plant in the hole. Set the crown of the plant at soil level, then back fill, firm and water in the plant.

ABOVE **A shaded area under a tree is the perfect place for hostas, primulas and astilbes, but they look even better if there is a water feature nearby.**

35

TREES, SHRUBS AND CLIMBERS

These are sold at every garden centre. Most are already growing in pots, and these do have many advantages over 'bare-root' plants (that is, plants that have been lifted from a nursery bed or field situation where they were growing in the ground). The first advantage is that they can be planted not only in winter, but right through the summer months. Remember, however, that planting anything during hot weather means that you must pay particular attention to watering. New plants that have not become established in the soil will quickly die if not watered after a few days of hot weather.

When choosing containerized woody plants do not be swayed by a fabulous display of flowers. Examine the plants to determine their states of health. Make sure their stems are healthy and strong, with no damage or disease. Try also to make sure that the plants are genuine container-grown plants, not bare-root specimens that have recently been potted up, perhaps hurriedly, for the nursery or garden centre to make a quick sale and get rid of them. You can tell if shrubs have been in their containers for the proper length of time by moss or algae on the soil surface – although an excess of this can also

ABOVE **Trees, shrubs and climbers are available for shade areas, but you will need to know what you are buying before you part with your money.**

indicate slapdash and undesirable practices in the nursery, where plant hygiene (that is, weeding and pest and diseases control) have been less than rigorous. Another way to identify how long a plant has been in a pot is to see if the roots are beginning to push through the holes in the base of the container. Most importantly, however, you should ask! If you go to a reliable nursery the staff there should be able to give you some useful and accurate information.

Most 'bare-root' plants are destined for sale in smaller plant nurseries, the thriving mail order plant businesses and in stores and supermarkets. In the case of the latter two, these bare-root plants are pre-packed and sealed, usually with some moisture kept around the roots by packing in moist tissue paper, or a small amount of compost.

If you really know what you are looking for, it is possible to get excellent plants in this way, and they are usually cheaper than container-grown types because you are not buying the pot and soil. You also have the advantage of seeing if the plant has a well-developed root system. Beware, however, of those with wrinkled, dried-up stems, or premature growth caused by high temperatures in transit, or in the shop, where the transparent packaging has created a mini 'greenhouse' around the plants, causing premature growth. This can also be a very good indication of the length of time the plant has been packed, and out of the ground. The hot atmosphere of a shop itself is rarely ideal – which is why cut-flower florists are usually very cool places – and so it is sensible to buy any such bare-root shrubs within just a few days of them appearing on the shelves.

Also, beware of specimens with spindly little shoots, or any that are discoloured with disease. Saleable plants should have a good, fibrous root system and a minimum of two strong, firm shoots, no thinner than a pencil, but preferably thicker.

ABOVE **Woodland plants such as *Pieris* (as well as rhododendrons, azaleas and camellias) make wonderful garden features.**

ABOVE Just before you set your plant in the ground, apply a dressing of blood, fish and bone, or bonemeal fertilizer.

ABOVE A stake should be used to support small trees; drive it into the hole before planting to avoid damaging the plant's roots.

Although bare-root trees, shrubs and climbers are available for much of the year, late autumn is the ideal time for planting them, and this is when nurseries and garden centres will be stocked to capacity with them. For the vast majority of trees, shrubs and climbers the soil needs to be free-draining, but moisture-retentive. This sounds like a contradiction, but in fact most soils do have these joint qualities.

If your soil is extremely sandy, and does not hold water well, you must incorporate plenty of humus into it before planting. This can be provided in the form of well-rotted garden compost or animal manure. Mix it well into the soil around and within the planting hole; do not plant any plants right into this material as it is too strong for the fine root hairs and will burn them. Make sure the compost or manure is mixed with the garden soil.

Similarly, if your soil is heavy clay, and water does not easily penetrate it and sits in muddy puddles on the surface, your plants will not appreciate this. So bulky organic matter as described should be used in this instance to break up the soil; to aid drainage, and provide valuable nutrition to what is likely to be an impoverished soil. Just before you set the plants in the ground, apply a dressing of bonemeal fertilizer over the area at the rate of 2oz per sq yd (65g per sq m). Work it in to the surface of the soil, using a hoe or rake, tread the area firm, and then rake it level.

Setting a climbing plant against a wall usually requires you to plant it 12in (30cm) or so away from the wall, in order to avoid the footings. In this case, make the hole and lay the plant at an angle, pointing towards the wall. Point the roots away from the wall, where the soil will often be dry, and towards moister soil. Water the climber in, and check it regularly for the first year, particularly during hot weather.

Container-grown trees, shrubs or climbers can be planted at any time of year, but if you are planting during the summer, or during a period of hot weather in spring or autumn, you must make sure to check for watering, almost on a daily basis, until such time as the general soil is consistently moist.

Just because container-grown plants have a neat root-ball when removed from the pot, do not be fooled into thinking that you simply need to dig a hole the same size as the root-ball, and then to drop it in. If you did this on a heavy clay soil you would be inadvertently creating a sump from which water would be slow to drain, and this could cause the roots to rot. It is a good idea, therefore, to break up the surrounding soil, and the base of the hole at planting time. Firm the plant in position, and water it in.

A stake should be used to support small trees, and it should be driven into the hole before planting, so as to avoid damaging the plant's roots. The top of the stake should come up just to the base of the first outward branches, to avoid unnecessary rubbing.

MAIL AND INTERNET ORDERED PLANTS

Many gardeners prefer to choose plants from a mail order catalogue. The main advantages of this method are that you can frequently find new, rare or unusual varieties; you don't need to leave the comfort of your armchair in order to make your selection (apart from the fact that you will need to go out and post your letter), and very often the plants will be cheaper than buying them from retail outlets.

The disadvantages to mail order purchasing of plants is that the colour reproduction in the catalogue may be some way off from the actual colouring of the flowers; and, most importantly, you do not get to see the quality of the plants before you part with your money. However, most bona fide nurseries offering a mail order service will want their reputation to remain intact, and so they should be happy to replace plants, or refund you, provided you complain as soon as the plants arrive, and you do not leave the plants for days or weeks before you make your claim.

These days the internet is a variation of the mail order business. The bigger nurseries will usually list the plants they stock, and usually show pictures in the 'catalogue' section of their websites. This is a much more immediate way to buy your plants (requiring you to use a credit or debit card to secure your purchases), but you are vulnerable to the same mail order disadvantages as those listed above.

ABOVE **Many gardeners prefer to buy their plants by mail order — each year hundreds of catalogues are produced by all the different nurseries that sell by this method.**

CHAPTER 4

Maintaining shade-loving plants

All plants need a certain amount of care and attention during the year if they are to give the best displays for our pleasure, and shade-loving plants are no exception. Feeding and watering are by far the most crucial requirements, but pruning is also an important element.

WATERING

All plants need water to survive and grow. It is important never to allow them to dry out completely. Even the sun-loving cacti and succulents need water to survive; it is just that they take in the little bit of moisture that is available and are able to store it effectively.

ABOVE **All plants need water to survive, but these days how you use the water, by using it wisely and without wasting it, is just as important.**

Once you have planted up your shade garden, watering is essential until the new plants have become established – and this could take two or even three years. Even then you should always water your plants during hot and dry spells. It is best carried out either early in the day or in the evening – both times when the sun is low in the sky and evaporation will be at its slowest. Remember that a good soaking of the soil every few days is better for plants and less wasteful of water than a mere splash around the leaves and stems twice a day.

It is a prerequisite of growing plants in containers, such as hanging baskets and windowboxes, that you have to look after them. They tend to dry out quickly as they are not in the ground, where there is more moisture available and they are often hung or placed in windy and exposed positions. Even a container placed in full shade will need watering most days during the summer months.

Automatic watering systems are now available that can easily be installed, to irrigate plants in the garden, and in containers. These devices are attached onto a mains water tap, and the pipes run along the areas for watering. A timer mechanism at the tap end is activated at a pre-set time and as a result, the plants and soil are watered for however long the device has been programmed.

The water exits from these pipes either through seep holes, or from stand-pipes with a jet nozzle to regulate the spray and its general direction of coverage. The former system, where water seeps through holes and soaks the ground, is generally accepted as the most efficient way to water, as there is very little evaporation, and moisture is not 'wasted' by getting it onto the plant leaves. Plants take up 99 per cent of their water via their roots, so it is here where any water given should be directed.

Less sophisticated watering comes in the form of traditional hosepipes and watering cans. These days, with threats of climate change and the likelihood of drier summers and more frequent droughts, it is economically and environmentally sensible to save as much rainwater as possible. I have four water butts and a colleague has thirteen! If you have the space, you can link the butts so that when one has filled, it overflows into the next. Although you cannot rig a hosepipe up to a water butt, you can fill countless cans of water. If you live on a water-metered property this will save you some money.

ABOVE **Direct water to the base of the plants as it is through the roots that most of the water is absorbed, not the leaves.**

MULCHING

In a shady garden mulches are of great importance, especially where the conditions are dry and the soil full of roots – such as under large trees. A mulch is a layer of material (organic or inorganic) applied around plants and on top of the soil surface. It has many benefits. The various materials include:

HOMEMADE COMPOST

Everyone should make their own compost, from garden and kitchen waste, mown grass clippings, shredded shrub and hedge trimmings and so on. Compost heaps and bins can convert these items of garden waste, in as little as six or seven months if the conditions are right, into usable, well-rotted material for using as a mulch. This particular material will hold water in the soil, preventing it from evaporating from around the plant's roots, and a thick layer will also provide protection for tender plants in cold weather.

LEAFMOULD

This is made from several layers of rotted leaves, collected together and compressed over several years. It is ideal for shade as it is nutrient-rich, adds fibre to the soil, improves drainage and helps to retain moisture. You can rarely find this to buy, however, which means that you will have to make your own, and if you do not have many broad-leaved trees close by, the raw material may not make this option very practicable.

FARMYARD MANURE

This is the ideal material to use if you want to feed the soil and maximize its moisture-retaining capabilities. Manure from horses and pigs is most commonly available, usually from farms which put up signs, but sometimes a town-based garden centre will be able to order it in for you. It is not particularly expensive but it is heavy and does not prevent weed growth – but it produces luxuriant plant growth

COMPOSTING TIP

Homemade compost from garden and kitchen waste, leafmould and farmyard manure should all be applied when they are well rotted. If it is applied in a raw state, its composite strength (acidic and high in ammonia) could damage the soil or any live plant material it touches. In fact, even in its well-rotted state, it should not be laid so that it touches the plants, as it will damage them.

ABOVE **Well-rotted homemade compost, made from garden and kitchen waste, grass clippings, and shredded woody material, is perfect for use as a mulch.**

ABOVE **Leafmould, made from layers of rotted leaves, and then compressed over several years, makes a good mulch and soil conditioner.**

ABOVE **Pulverized or shredded bark, when used as a mulch, will conserve soil moisture and help to prevent weed growth.**

BARK

This is, perhaps, the most popular of today's modern mulching materials. It is relatively cheap, light, and biodegradable and has good weed-suppressing and moisture-retaining qualities. Bark is available in 'pulverized', 'shredded' and 'chipped' forms, and in colours other than 'natural'. In commercial landscaping the greens, golds and black bark chips are highly popular, but for domestic gardens the tendency is usually to go for something more natural in colour. The downside to using bark is that it needs regularly topping up, and its appearance is not always to everyone's taste. It also removes nitrogen from the soil as it rots down, which is a drawback as this element is required for good plant growth.

STONE CHIPPINGS AND GRAVEL

These are long lasting and there is a huge range of colours and size grades to choose from. For a shady garden, however, there are more downsides than upsides to using gravel and stone. To start with, in the autumn when leaves fall it is difficult to sweep or clear the area. Also, if sunlight does not regularly fall on gravel it can turn green with algae or moss growth. A thin layer of gravel will afford some moisture retention in the soil, but to do this effectively the layer should be 3in (7.5cm) or more. No matter how thick a gravel mulch, weeds will always seem to germinate in it, but fortunately they are usually quite easy to remove. Chipped slate, in plum, blue or grey shades is a popular alternative to natural yellowish or brown gravel.

CRUSHED GLASS

Modern garden designers use this material extensively in their contemporary schemes. It is a relatively new material, and is available in a range of bright colours. Despite the fact that it is glass, it is safe as the sharp edges have been rounded off during the manufacturing process. It has similar qualities to gravel, but is much more expensive and does not always blend well with the planting schemes in traditional gardens.

ABOVE **Coloured glass chippings can be used as a mulch in contemporary gardens and planting schemes.**

ABOVE **Traditional gravel (there are various sizes and grades you can choose) makes a good mulch for small beds and rockeries, but it is not a soil conditioner.**

FEEDING

Plants growing in a shady spot are likely to need more feeding than those growing in the open, or in full sun for the following reasons:

1 The lack of sunlight will be putting a plant under a degree of stress, so it is important to make sure that it gets a regular supply of nourishment from the soil.

2 The shade is most likely to be caused by nearby trees, hedges or large shrubs, which greedily gobble what nutrition there is in the soil. Or if buildings are the cause of the shade, the foundations, footings or other structures (such as sewerage pipes, water mains and so on) can interfere with the structure of the soil, and the goodness it contains.

3 Some plants may be reluctant to flower if they are growing in the shade. This can, in part, be helped by providing fertilizers that are proportionately higher in potassium such as tomato or rose fertilizers, which are designed to promote flowering.

Of course, plants grown directly in the ground will require less feeding than those growing in pots or containers. However, soil in dry shade is often particularly hungry. The best course of action is to provide annual mulches of manure in early spring. As well as helping to retain water it will feed the plants. Between mulches, it is a good idea to supplement the feeding by applying granular or pelleted chicken manure, which is strong, effective and easy to apply – if a little smelly at first. Also in spring, inorganic balanced fertilizers, such as Growmore, can be applied according to the manufacturers' recommendations, then lightly hoed or forked in.

ABOVE **Plants growing in the shade will need slightly more feed than those growing in the open, or in full sun.**

PRUNING

There are seven main reasons why we prune plants, particularly those growing in shade:

1 Keeping plants to size
2 Maintaining shape and habit
3 Removing unwanted growth
4 Improving flowering
5 Improving fruiting
6 Improving foliage and stems
7 Treating pests and diseases

KEEPING PLANTS TO SIZE

Because of pressures of space and modern living these days, most of us are faced with smaller gardens than were enjoyed by our ancestors. Therefore it has become essential either to select and grow plants that will achieve a modest size when fully developed, or to ensure that we limit the size of larger subjects by keeping them under control. In other words, pruning them carefully so that they do not grow too big for the space allocated to them.

MAINTAINING SHAPE AND HABIT

Most trees and shrubs look their best when they are allowed to grow naturally; in a natural setting it is always best, wherever possible, to retain a plant's natural shape. Trained plants, or those trimmed to a formal shape, are exceptions to this. However, even in a natural and informal setting vigorous shoots can upset the balance. Plants growing in the shade can very often throw out awkwardly placed shoots searching for light. Any such growths should be cut out.

ABOVE **Pruning plants is the only way to remove growth that is unwanted — perhaps it is diseased, damaged, dead or just in the wrong place.**

Shrubs that have grown out of balance can be reshaped if these general guidelines are followed:

1 Remove straggling branches to a shoot or bud within the main bulk of the plant.
2 Carefully but systematically reduce the number of growths on the 'good' side of the plant.
3 Cut back weak shoots hard, and strong shoots lightly on the 'bad' side of the plant.
4 Feed the plant with a good general fertilizer.
5 Mulch with compost or manure.

REMOVING UNWANTED GROWTH

Plants that are not maintained – that is, pruned regularly or at least annually – can often become a dense mass of tangled branches. This means that the shoots in the middle of the mass are deprived of light and air, and are prone to dying back. During windy weather the stems can rub together, causing injury to themselves and the branches they are rubbing against. All of these conditions lead to a greatly increased risk of disease.

ABOVE **Some pruning is specifically done to encourage flowering, such as with this wisteria, being trained along a house front.**

IMPROVING FLOWERING

This reason for pruning can be particularly important in a shade situation. Decoration is what gardening is all about, and we would be failing, as gardeners, were we to allow trees, shrubs and other plants, to produce less than their optimum decorative effect. Usually, the more flowers a plant produces, the smaller they become. Pruning therefore reduces the amount of wood, and so diverts energy into the production of larger, though fewer, flowers.

IMPROVING FRUITING

It generally follows that flowers ultimately lead to fruit. Therefore, if you are wanting to maximize a plant's potential for fruiting, more or less the same pruning guidelines as for flowering plants apply: to continually aim to encourage productive growth. It is quite difficult, but not unheard of, to get plants growing in the shade to bear fruit.

Farmers and gardeners alike always desire the largest possible crops, but where fruit is concerned there can come a time when the plant bears too many fruits, all of which are small. If the crop is thinned out – another form of pruning – well before ripening, the individual fruits will be appreciably larger.

IMPROVING FOLIAGE AND STEMS

The rule of thumb here is that leaves are produced only on current season's growth. Therefore the more vigorous this is, the larger and more profuse will be the foliage. Also, in plants with coloured leaves, the hues will be more vivid and intense. For this reason, many vigorous shrubs grown for their foliage are pruned hard annually. And this is particularly key to shade-grown plants. In the shade, variegations and other leaf colours are less vivid. More reversion (where a plant with variegated leaves produces stems with all-green leaves) takes place, too.

ABOVE *Cornus sericea* 'Flaviramea' (AGM) shows its colourful stems in winter, but only if it is pruned in early spring.

Green shoots should be cut out, right to their base. These reverted growths tend to be more vigorous than the rest of the plant, and if left to their own devices will take over, spoiling the overall appearance of the plant. Some deciduous shrubs, such as *Cornus alba* (dogwood) and *Salix alba vitellina* (willow), have coloured barks, and are grown purposely to enhance the winter garden. The most effective colour is produced on young stems, so these shrubs should be cut as close to the ground as possible in early spring.

TREATING PESTS AND DISEASES
The following are gardening troubles that can be wholly or partly treated by pruning.

Pest or disease	Description	Pruning action
Aphids	blackfly, greenfly, etc	pinch out affected shoots or leaves
Brown rot	found on apples and pears	remove all mummified, or rotten, fruits remaining on the tree after harvesting
Canker	found on apples and pears	cut out infected wood
Caterpillars	bore into stems	cut out infected branches
Coral spot	disease of dead wood on various trees and shrubs	remove to healthy wood
Fire blight	disease of trees and shrubs from the rose family	remove to healthy wood
Leaf miners	insect pests that burrow under the leaf layers of plants	pick off affected leaves
Powdery mildew	disease found on various plants	pinch out, or cut away affected growth
Silverleaf	disease of certain fruit trees, including cherry trees, almond trees, etc	cut out infected wood before mid-summer
Woolly aphid	insect pest found on various fruit trees	cut out badly infected wood

OTHER KINDS OF PRUNING

Some jobs carried out in a garden are forms of pruning, although they are hardly recognized as such:

Deadheading: All cultivated flowering plants should be deadheaded – the removal of faded flowers before the plant has created the seed that follows. By doing this you are saving a huge amount of wasted energy, and it can either encourage more flowers in the same year, or help to build up the plant for better flowering the following year. Generally with woody plants the recommendation is to use a pair of secateurs, and to cut off the faded flowers, cutting the stalks down as far as the first set of leaves. As always there are exceptions. Rhododendrons, for example, should have their old flowerheads snapped off by your fingers. Bedding plants and some soft perennials can be deadheaded and this may be best done with fingers, or a pair of shears (as you would with, say, lavender).

Cutting the lawn: Trimming grass is pruning – one is simply reducing the size of individual grass plants. Remember that lawns sited in the shade are under much greater stress than those sited in full sun, so they should be mown less frequently.

Cutting stems of flowers for decoration: Cut a sprig of flowers for home decoration, particularly from a woody plant, and you are simply pruning the plant whilst it is in flower. You should endeavour to follow the rules of pruning, by using a sharp cutting tool, and cutting above a bud, preferably one that is facing out from the centre of the plant.

Cutting back perennials: At the end of the growing year a perennial border should be tidied up. Old, dying topgrowth should be cut back to ground level (unless seedheads are required for winter decoration). Try to remove stems as close to the crown of the plant as possible. Perennials treated in this fashion are being 'pruned'.

Tree surgery: This is an extreme form of pruning, usually done to maintain a mature tree in a healthy condition. Because powered saws or working high up in the tree are frequently required, it is a sensible option here to employ the services of a professional tree surgeon who will be skilled and insured.

ABOVE Cutting the grass is a form of 'pruning'! But remember that lawns in shade are under greater stress than those in full sun, so they should be mown less frequently.

ABOVE Deadheading is important for all flowering plants – from large woody rhododendrons and border roses, through to bedding plants and even small Gold Lace primulas, as seen here.

SUPPORTING

Many herbaceous plants that re-grow annually will require some form of support to prevent them flopping over other plants, or in on themselves. Tie them to bamboo canes, or buy purpose-made wire hoop supports that are pushed in the ground for the plant to grow up and through. These should be put in position in the early to mid-spring period, before the plants start growing apace. Some shrubs may require more support, using stakes or canes as they grow.

Climbers need to be trained to trelliswork. As new stems on these plants develop, they should be tied in to their supports, to avoid wind damage. If this is done regularly, they should be in position to replace any older wood that can be pruned out at the appropriate pruning time. If they are left untied they may break, get in the way (of a path or patio, for example), or at least become inflexible enough to make tying in later on more difficult.

ABOVE **Climbing plants will sometimes adhere to or ramble over vertical surfaces, but more often than not they will need some supporting mechanism, such as trellis panels, particularly during their formative growing period.**

CHAPTER 5

Weeds, pests and diseases

All plants are susceptible to pests and diseases and just because plants growing in the shade may not be immediately as evident or as prominent as those growing in full sun, they are every bit as vulnerable. There are, to help us out, an increasing number of new plant varieties that are being bred for resistance to certain diseases, and unlike 50 years ago there are some very effective controls available today.

The best way to prevent pests and diseases is to practise good husbandry – a lovely old gardening term, meaning to cultivate sensibly and 'hygienically'. In gardening, the word 'hygiene' is used in the context of keeping an area clean of unwanted plants, weeds, moss, algae and debris, all of which could be the breeding grounds for pests and diseases.

WEED CONTROL

You should keep your garden as free from weeds as possible. Unfortunately, there is no simple, magical cure for the problem of weeds, but the important thing to realize is that by allowing them to grow, you will, unwittingly, be encouraging a number of pests and diseases to get a hold. Many types will become host plants for the breeding of aphids, and others make the ideal homes for diseases like rust and mildew. The easiest weeds to control are annuals, which are best kept in check by hoeing, mulching and spraying. More troublesome, however, are the

ABOVE **Weeds will soon take over a patch of ground. Although fewer weeds tend to grow in shady conditions, there are still plenty that will.**

perennial weeds, such as ground elder, couch grass (or twitch), bindweed, docks, thistles and perennial nettles. These will all come up year after year if left to their own devices.

When you are first setting out plants in your shade border, you should make sure that the ground is completely weed-free, particularly important if there are perennial weeds present, such as those mentioned above. If you have an area covered with, for example, couch grass, the best course of action is to spray the area with a herbicide based on glyphosate, which will kill all parts of the plant it is sprayed on to.

Happily, the chemical becomes inactive on contact with the soil, and it is not taken up by the roots of any plant, no matter how close to the area of spray.

WEED SEED CONTROL

To control new weed seedlings from appearing amongst the plants in your shade garden, use only those products that are probably based on simazine and that carry the manufacturer's recommendations for use with ornamental or edible plants. Apply in spring, when the soil is firm and moist. The chemical acts as a sort of sealant over the surface of the soil, preventing weed seeds from germinating. It should remain active throughout the whole growing season.

METHOD

1 Before applying, remove any weeds by hand. Or, if they are very small, hoe lightly or apply a contact weedkiller such as paraquat. But be careful to avoid letting this chemical come into contact with the plants you are growing.
2 Prune and feed the plants as required.
3 Apply the simazine-based control.
4 Finish by applying a mulch (see p42–43).

ABOVE **Groundsel, a ragged, rather untidy-looking plant, with its many-branched upright stems, is a common inhabitant of shaded ground.**

ABOVE **Chickweed, although an annual, is difficult to eradicate by hand as, when pulled, it snaps off at soil level and re-grows readily.**

ABOVE Dandelions are one of the commonest of perennial weeds; the only way to ensure eradication by hand is to dig out the root, removing all parts of it.

PERENNIAL WEED CONTROL

It is always best to remove these by hand, digging out as much of the root as possible. However, if there are large areas covered with them, or if there are holly plants or others with nasty thorns or spikes and you do not fancy braving them to get in and tackle the weeds at close quarters, you could spray with a weedkiller based on dichlobenil. Apply when the soil is moist, and in spring, before the leaves start to unfurl.

At the rates at which it can safely be used near woody plants, some perennial weeds (such as ground elder and couch grass) will be checked or progressively controlled. Other, deeper-rooting weeds may not be checked sufficiently to see them off, so hand-weeding is best for these. Dichlobenil will also control germinating weed seedlings and established annual weeds for up to six months after application.

If couch and other grass weeds are your main problem, apply a weedkiller based on alloxydim-sodium. It is foliage-acting, non-residual and harmless to non-grassy plants, so it will not matter if you inadvertently get some on your shrubs.

PESTS

There is a huge variety of insect pests that prey on garden plants, and they are prevalent more in some countries than others. But the three most common types are aphids, thrips and sawfly.

SLUGS AND SNAILS

These are, for many, the number one garden pest. They are arguably more of a danger in a shady garden, too, as these slimy molluscs do not like the sun. They hide and lurk under stones and patio pots, away from the glare, and some species live in the soil itself. They like damp but not sodden positions, and their favourite foods are the soft, fleshy leaves and stems of seedlings, some bedding plants and soft perennials such as hostas.

You can buy nasty, poisonous baits based on metaldehyde or methiocarb, but as a matter of personal choice I stopped using these years ago. I have tried the old wives' tales of putting down orange peel (which attracts them in

ABOVE There are many different species of slug and, between them, they will all devour our favourite plants: although they tend not to eat the weeds, for some reason!

numbers where they can be collected and disposed of in a manner of your choosing), and also beer traps, where they are lured into a slop-trough of beer, get drunk and drown. Both of these have had mixed success.

A couple of years ago I tried biological controls – nematodes – that you water onto the soil around susceptible plants. This was one of the most successful forms of control I've come across. The reason for my caution, however, is that controlling them 'biologically' in this way is expensive, and you're never quite sure of the success rate. There are one or two hostas in pots that I have determined should not be attacked, so I shall scatter a few handfuls of crushed eggshells around the bases. This, at least for me, has worked surprisingly well in the past.

APHIDS

These are the greenfly or blackfly that we see around the garden, infesting a whole range of garden plants. The aphids that attack your flowering currants, or broad beans, or mock oranges may be slightly different species of aphid, but the insects are not always fussy as to the type of plant they feed off, so all should be controlled as soon as they are seen.

Aphids feed by sucking the sap of young, tender plant growths. They are often seen clustering on young, unopened buds, and also on the undersides of young leaves. Their feeding will not kill an established plant, unless it is very small, but it will distort the buds and leaves, which can certainly ruin the appearance and flowering potential. Aphids also excrete honeydew, which attracts an unsightly black fungus called sooty mould. Again, this looks unsightly and in severe cases will debilitate a plant, but not actually kill it.

Small infestations of aphids should be cut away, and the infested parts thrown in the bin. Larger infestations should be sprayed. There are many insecticides and modern systemic aphicides available today, and they all vary

ABOVE **Crushed eggshells, if placed around plants (in pots or in the ground), can sometimes be offputting to slugs and snails, affording a little more protection to your plants.**

ABOVE **Blackfly (and greenfly) infest a whole range of garden plants, and should be controlled as soon as they are seen. They are known to carry viral infections from plant to plant.**

slightly in their formulations and prices. A typical garden centre or shop will have a selection, and you should read the labels to decide on the best product for your situation.

OTHER INSECT PESTS

Amongst a plethora of other potential insect pests that attach to our garden plants, the following four are probably the most common:

Vine weevils: Plants growing in pots or other containers, out of doors or under cover, can be severely affected by vine weevil grubs. Plants

ABOVE Vine weevil adults are commonly found around garden plants, but it is the little white grubs under the soil that do most damage.

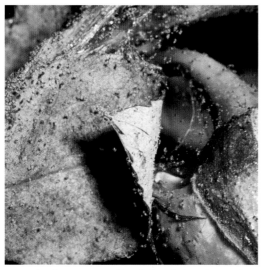

ABOVE Red spider mites are visible with the naked eye, but it is the very fine webbing between the stems and the leaves that are likely to be noticed first.

growing in the open ground are less likely to be damaged, although the grubs sometimes kill strawberries, forms of *Primula*, *Cyclamen*, *Sedum*, *Heuchera* and young yew plants. Irregular-shaped notches are eaten in leaf margins by the adult weevils during the summer. Plants wilt and die during autumn to spring as a result of grubs devouring the roots.

Thrips: These are small, narrow-bodied sap-sucking insects. They feed on the flowers of certain plants, both as the grubs (larvae) and as winged adults. The larvae dig deep into the buds and eat the petal tissues inside. If, when a flower bud opens and you notice that the expanding petals are deformed and damaged, the plant will most certainly be suffering with thrips. The adults are carried on the wind and seem more attracted to pale-coloured blooms – such as whites, creams and pale pinks.

Controlling this pest is not easy. Natural predators are seldom enough to control thrips, as the little pests spend much of their time buried deep inside a flower or bud, and out of sight – where chemicals can't easily get to them. Insecticides are available, however, and some control is provided when treating for other insects, such as aphids.

Caterpillars: There are a number of different caterpillar species that will readily devour foliage. One of the worst is the caterpillar of the winter moth, seen as bright green caterpillars some ½in (1cm) long. If they are not too numerous, pick them off by hand. Otherwise, spray with a suitable insecticide.

Red spider mites: These cause bronze patches on the upper surfaces of leaves, and you will more than likely find very fine webbing between the leaves and stems. The spiders are minute and distinctly yellowish rather than red. Attacks are worst in hot, dry weather. Chemical control of spider mites is possible and works well.

ABOVE Most species of butterfly and moth have caterpillars as their larval stage, and nearly all will be pests of garden plants at some point. Spray against them, but only on the plants you do not wish to have damaged.

Leaf miners: These attack a range of garden plants, from chrysanthemums to holly, and also some vegetables. Yellowish or yellowish-purple blotches occur on the upper surface of the older leaves, usually near the centre of the leaf. Insecticides are not always effective as the surface of the leaves often means that sprays run off the foliage and do not penetrate to where the grubs are feeding. On small specimen plants it is feasible to remove mined leaves but not if this would result in significant defoliation.

NON-INSECT PESTS

You could argue that children who trample over gardens, or vandals, or wayward vehicles that scrape or crash into our plants inadvertently are 'pests', but normally when referring to non-insect plant pests we are referring to marauding birds and mammals.

Birds: The damage they cause usually comes in the form of fruit-eating. Blackbirds can strip a holly tree of berries in a matter of a few hours – and just a week or two before Christmas as well, which is most frustrating. Other birds break in to ripening apples on the trees. Birds can also eat buds and nibble away at foliage, but these are of lesser importance.

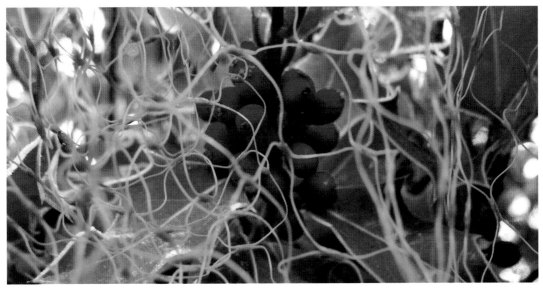

ABOVE Birds will quickly devour many of our autumn and winter berries, particularly if the weather is cold; prevent them from stripping the plants by draping netting over the plants, but arrange it in such a way that it does not trap birds.

It is, however, generally recommended that gardeners encourage birds into their gardens as they also bring many benefits. Some species (such as thrushes) will devour slugs and snails. Others (including many of the sparrows and tit families) gobble up aphids and other small crawlers. And, let's not forget, that birds are also great to watch when they're feeding from a well-placed bird table.

Mammals: Rabbits, deer and voles are the worst offenders, especially if you live in a rural location. The rabbit will frequently munch its way through a border of young and emerging perennial plants during springtime. Deer will devour stems, buds, leaves and bark of young trees, and so will voles. Tree guards, made from plastic and usually in green, brown or white, and metal tree protectors are useful for keeping the larger animals away. Special low vole guards are also available.

ABOVE Tree guards and shelters are commonly used in large planting schemes where many valuable trees are at risk of damage by rabbits, deer and other mammals; these products can be used in domestic gardens as well.

ABOVE Most plants in our gardens are susceptible to damage by rabbits – which are at their most active in late winter and spring.

ABOVE Deer are almost exclusively a pest of rural gardens, where they will strip trees of bark, young shoots and leaves.

PLANT DISEASES

Plant diseases can often have some quite ugly sounding names. There's 'blossom end rot' (tomatoes), 'scab' (apples, pears, potatoes and many others), 'blackleg' (potatoes), 'club root' (which affects members of the cabbage family), as well as various 'blights', 'spots', 'mildews', 'moulds' and 'rusts'!

There are nicer sounding diseases as well, but they are just as critical when it comes to the health of the plants. There is, for example, 'silver leaf' (which affects fruit tree leaves), 'honey fungus' and 'coral spot' (many woody plants) and 'peach leaf curl' (mainly peaches).

Actually, fungi cause most plant diseases. The invisible fungal spores travel through the air, soil or water, spreading their growth. These spores come from the 'fruiting bodies' of the fungus, which in the case of mushrooms and toadstools are the mushrooms and toadstools! Different fungi have very different fruiting bodies. Mildew, for example, spreads its spores by the familiar white coating on leaves, resembling a fine layer of sieved talcum powder.

With many fungal diseases you can visibly see the spread – honey fungus, for example, shows a white 'mycelium', a thread-like mass of filaments or strands that forms the vegetative part of the fungus.

TROUBLESOME DISEASES AND HOW TO CONTROL THEM

Mildew: There are two different types of mildew. The first, and more pertinent, form is powdery mildew, identified by the way it covers young leaves, buds and stems by its white 'mycelium'. Older parts of the plant are generally resistant to mildew. Without treatment, the disease will cause the affected parts to become stunted and distorted. The spores are carried on the wind, and they will most readily infest plants that are slightly dehydrated, or if there is poor air circulation in the vicinity of the plant, such as with climbing roses growing

ABOVE **Powdery mildew is more of a problem on plants during prolonged hot and dry weather, when plants are more vulnerable to attack by the fungus.**

against walls (these types of rose, in general, are more susceptible, for this reason). Cool, wet weather makes the ideal conditions for the spores to germinate. The second type of mildew is known as downy mildew, which is characterized by greyish brown pustules on the undersides of the leaves.

Rust: A wide variety of plants are affected by rust but some of the most common are broad beans, roses, chrysanthemums, pelargoniums and fuchsias. The early signs of a rust infection are irregular discolouration on the foliage and stem. On closer inspection these are often circular in appearance and usually correspond to dark orange, brown, yellow or red spots or pustules on the undersides of the leaves. Chemical sprays are available, but severely infected plants should be lifted and burnt – not composted as this will perpetuate the disease.

ABOVE Botrytis (or greymould) disease attacks stems, leaves and flowers, and is worse during damp, cool and still conditions. A furry grey coating develops over the plant, and will cause it to die if the infection is severe.

Botrytis: Also known as greymould disease, it forms a grey mould on leaves, stems and flowers, and thrives in cool, damp, still air – the sort of place that most unheated greenhouses possess in winter. Any plants you are keeping under glass over winter are vulnerable. Increase ventilation so that there is some movement of air and don't splash water about.

Bacteria: Various bacteria also have their evil way with our greenery. These are much smaller than fungi, being only just visible with an ordinary microscope. Infection invariably enters a plant through a wound or opening. 'Bacterial canker' is a serious disease of cherries, plums and other stone fruit, and symptoms include oozing gum from the bark.

USING SPRAYS

Fungicidal sprays are available but, as stated earlier, plants with the best health are most likely to avoid infection. Pay particular attention to watering the plants, particularly in times of drought. When applying pesticides and herbicides, it is most important that they are distributed both accurately and uniformly. Not only does this ensure the safety of the plants, but is it also what I call the three 'E's: the most effective, the most economical and most environmentally-appropriate approach.

Organic gardeners, who choose not to use any form of man-made chemical to control such things as garden pests and diseases have created a bit of a problem for themselves. However, a combination of being vigilant (nipping out diseased leaves and buds when seen) and using products approved by the various organic bodies and institutes in the countries where you live when only absolutely necessary, are probably the best ways forward.

ABOVE The rule when spraying is not to spray indiscriminately; only do it in the evening or early morning, and not when pollinating insects are about.

Viruses: These are even more insidious as you can't cure them. Most are introduced into plants by pests – particularly greenfly and eelworms (which is why it is so important to control these insects). Once infection occurs nearly every cell of a diseased plant becomes infected, and there is no method by which a gardener can cure such a plant, so it should be destroyed (preferably by burning as this gets rid of the virus; simply putting a virused plant on the compost heap could perpetuate the problem).

It therefore follows that 'fungicides' are the chemical products specifically designed to cure, or to halt the progress, of fungal diseases. Insecticides are different, in that they are designed to kill insects, which eat, burrow or infest our plants. Together, fungicides and insecticides are known as 'pesticides'.

SPRAYING GUIDELINES
1 Only spray on a still day, for spray drift caused by the wind can cause havoc.
2 If possible, spray in early morning or in the evening, as this is when flying insects are most inactive; bees and other beneficial creatures can sometimes be harmed by these chemicals, and it is the responsibility of all of us to avoid indiscriminate harm to them.
3 Carefully follow the instructions from the manufacturer when it comes to mixing, dosage and application; large amounts of concentrated chemicals can harm plants, soil and animal life, and therefore be unpleasant for all of us.

CHAPTER 6

Year-round care

This chapter could be the most thumbed-through chapter of the book, as within it you will discover precisely when you need to be doing things to – and in – your shade garden and borders.

The gardening year is divided into 12; by all means think of them as 'months', but I am not going to label them 'January', 'February', and so on. Depending on where you live, and from year-to-year, the weather for, say, October may be considerably warmer for you than another reader at the opposite end of the country. So it is far more accurate to refer to the 12 divisions seasonally.

Regardless of this palaver, if you put into practice the information contained here, your shady areas of the garden will give you optimum performance, year in year out.

ABOVE Gardens with a large amount of shade generate just as many 'jobs to do' as bright, sunny gardens.

ABOVE **Plant hardy trees, shrubs or perennials in early winter, provided the ground is not frozen or waterlogged.**

ABOVE **Prune shade-loving climbing roses growing on wires or fences; but do not prune ramblers at this time (they should be pruned in late summer).**

EARLY WINTER

Dig the soil: New shade beds and borders may be dug, and old ones renovated, in time for any new plants you intend to acquire. The soil needs time to settle, so do not do any planting yet.

Planting: Having said that, new hardy shrubs may be planted, on a day when the soil is not frozen or waterlogged, on ground that has been prepared a month or two previously. But before you dig the holes and plant them, give the area a final application of bonemeal fertilizer at 2oz per sq yd (65g per sq m), working this into the surface, treading the ground firm and then raking it level.

Forcing rhubarb and seakale: There are few vegetables that thrive in a shade garden (see p152–155), but rhubarb and seakale can be grown with some success. This is a good time to start forcing them outdoors. Provide complete darkness by placing a cover, such as a large bucket, old barrel, plastic drum or even a purpose-made 'forcing pot' over the top of the crowns of the plants. After five or six weeks the cover can be removed, to expose blanched, tender sticks for taking straight into the kitchen.

MID-WINTER

Planting: Hardy trees, shrubs, perennials and climbers may be planted in soil that was prepared a month or two previously; it should be dressed with fertilizer (as detailed above) just prior to planting.

Prick over bulbs beds: Tulips, daffodils and hyacinths and other spring bulbs will be appearing through the soil now. As soon as the green sprouts can be seen clearly, go over the beds carefully with a small border fork, pricking the soil between the bulbs, but only to the depth of about 1in (2.5cm). This helps to improve aeration around the roots, kill moss and loosen weeds for removal.

Pruning climbing roses: Some climbing roses growing on shaded walls may be pruned at this time; leave ramblers until late summer. Thriving plants will have produced a number of strong shoots during the previous summer, and the aim should be to keep five to seven strong, well-placed growths. Remove as many as possible of the older stems that have flowered.

ABOVE Cut back the old flowered stems of bush or mophead hydrangeas (*Hydrangea macrophylla*) in late winter.

ABOVE Early spring is the best time to divide many perennials and, as seen here, chives from the vegetable or herb garden.

LATE WINTER

Prune flowering shrubs: Shade-loving flowering shrubs that should be pruned now include the climbing hydrangea (*Hydrangea petiolaris*) and mophead type (*Hydrangea macrophylla*), the Rose of Sharon (*Hypericum calycinum*) and also the colour-stemmed dogwood (*Cornus alba*). In all these plants, stems made the previous year should be cut back hard to within one or two joints of the older wood.

Weed and pest control: After pruning, weed the beds thoroughly.

Control rabbits: Damage to your trees and shrubs by rabbits can be very significant, particularly if you live in a rural area. The main damage is caused to the fresh growths that emerge after pruning. You may wish to erect a barrier of wire netting, some 3ft (90cm) high around your plants at this time. Turn the bottom 6in (15cm) of the wire mesh outwards, and bury it under the soil or turf. This will help to safeguard your plants. It is advisable to leave the barrier in place until the worst of the rabbit activity is past (after about two months).

EARLY SPRING

Apply fertilizer: Plants set in well-manured soil do not require a dressing of fertilizer in spring. Established plants, however, should be given a feed, using a balanced fertilizer. Always check the manufacturers' application rates on the side of the packet. Rake or hoe the feed into the top inch or two of the soil.

Mulching: Once border plants have started into growth, and the soil has become warmer, a mulch of organic material will help to nourish them, conserve moisture in the soil and suppress weed growth. Cow or horse manure, spent mushroom or normal garden compost may be used, but in every case it must be well rotted. A layer 2–3in (5–8cm) deep is needed for effective results; do not allow the material to lay against the stems of the plants, as it may 'burn' the plant tissue. Wait until the soil is moist after rain before applying it.

Dividing plants: This is the best time to transplant the majority of herbaceous plants. When transplanting old clumps always break them up into smaller pieces, and if you have plenty of stock throw away the hard central portions, keeping only the outside pieces. Chives, growing in the vegetable or herb garden, can also be split at this time.

ABOVE Spray to get rid of weeds. This can be done throughout the growing season but is most important at the start, in spring, before the flowers have set seed.

MID-SPRING

Feed lawns: Grass that is predominately in the shade should be fed twice a year: once now, using a proprietary lawn fertilizer formulated for spring/summer use, and again in the autumn. Shaded grass is under stress, so it is important also to aerate the soil – spiking the area with a garden fork to a depth of about 6in (15cm). This is particularly important under large trees.

Late planting: There is still time to replace any plants that were damaged or killed during the winter. At this time of year you should plant only container-grown varieties, as they can be placed into the planting holes without any disturbance to the roots.

Pests and diseases: Continue to look for and control aphids. These insects breed at an alarming rate unless they are spotted at an early stage and action taken immediately.

Weeding: The mulching described for early spring will go a long way to controlling weeds in your beds and borders. Failing this, however, you will need to weed by hand, or with the use of chemicals. In either case, a concerted effort now will pay dividends later; effective weed control in early spring will result in fewer weeds setting seed.

ABOVE Layering is a convenient way to propagate many shade-loving shrubs, including rhododendrons and, as seen here, ivies.

LATE SPRING

Propagate by layering: Layering is a simple method of propagating quite a number of shade-loving plants, including rhododendrons and ivies (forms of *Hedera*). Choose a good, supple branch or stem, preferably one formed the previous year; make an upward incision through one of its joints, not too near the tip but at a point that can easily be bent down to soil level, press the cut portion of the stem into the soil (or a pot filled with cuttings compost), and hold it in position with a wire peg or heavy stone. After six to eight months roots should have formed and this section can then be severed from the main plant.

Tie in climbers: As new stems on these plants develop, they should be tied in to their supports, to avoid wind damage. If this is done regularly, they should be in position to replace the older wood, which can be pruned out during the following mid-winter. Left untied they may well break, or at least be inflexible enough to make tying in later on more difficult.

Pests and diseases: Continue keeping a watchful eye for signs of infestation or infection: never let plants, pests or diseases gain a firm hold. Spray as necessary.

Remove suckers: Suckers come from below the graft union of roses, plums, sumachs and many other suckering garden plants. They frequently have greater vigour than the main plants and, if left, will take over. Suckers must be removed whenever they are seen, but they will become most evident during this period.

Plant up containers: Plant up summer-flowering annuals in hanging baskets and patio planters. Try to keep these in the sunniest places possible until they become completely settled and established. See mid-summer.

EARLY SUMMER

Pests and diseases: Aphids will be troublesome around now. The larvae of various caterpillars eat leaf, stem and flower tissue, reducing them to skeletons. Red spider mite can infect fruit trees at this time. For all these pests you should spray now. Also, spray the top and undersides of leaves with a fungicide as a precaution against mildew. Once the white mildew appears, spraying is ineffective.

Feeding: Unless your soil is particularly fertile, established plants will benefit from another application of fertilizer. A balanced, general feed at a rate of 2 oz per sq yd (65g per sq m) will encourage blooms. Do not apply this feed beyond early summer, as it will promote growth of young stems that will not ripen before the onset of colder weather.

Hedges: Evergreen hedges can be trimmed now that nesting birds have moved on.

Making notes: As you travel about you will see many plants in shaded parts of people's gardens, and many will be in flower. Take note of names – when possible – of types you like, for reading up about and perhaps ordering later. Think about copying ideas or making changes to the garden in the following winter. It is often better to visualize changes when plants are at their most colourful.

LEFT Evergreen hedges can be trimmed in early summer, after nesting birds have moved on.

MID-SUMMER

Containers: The spring-planted hanging baskets and patio planters can be placed into the shady part of the garden now, and kept there for the remainder of the summer.

Prune flowering shrubs: Shrubs that flowered during mid- to late spring can be pruned now, but this is not to say that pruning is always necessary. Much depends upon the purpose for which the shrub is being grown and the amount of space that you can spare it. For example, lilacs, rhododendrons, azaleas, pieris and camellias need no regular pruning of a severe nature. *Clematis montana* may be cut back sufficiently to keep it within bounds.

Deadheading: It is a great advantage to remove the faded flower trusses of any flowering plants, so preventing the formation of seed, and the wasting of energy therefore.

Tie in climbing roses: Continue to do this (see late spring).

Cut back perennials: *Aubrieta*, *Arabis* and *Iberis* (perennial candytuft) may be cut back considerably when they have finished flowering if you wish to stop the plants from spreading.

Pests and diseases: Continue to control (see early summer). Aphids may be less of a problem from now, but rose rust may be starting now.

ABOVE **In early to mid-summer patio planters and hanging baskets can be moved into a shady part of the garden to brighten it up.**

ABOVE **Most flowering plants, including roses, should be deadheaded, to save the plants' energy and to prevent unwanted seeds forming.**

ABOVE **Continue to control aphids until mid-autumn, after which chemical controls become ineffective.**

LATE SUMMER

Prune rambler roses: Late summer and into early autumn is the best time for pruning ramblers growing on sunless walls and fences. First untie all the stems from the supports so that you can see what's what.

Ordering new bulbs: Around now all of the specialist bulb nurseries are bringing out their mail order catalogues for the forthcoming year. Choose your plants and place your orders early, particularly if you are wanting newly launched varieties, as stocks may run out.

Deadheading: Continue to remove faded flowerheads (see early summer).

Pests and diseases: Continue to control them (see early summer).

Trim hedges: Continue to trim evergreen hedges and topiary specimens as necessary to keep them neat and tidy.

Containers: Refresh containers, replacing any summer-flowering plants that may have finished. Make sure the containers are always well watered, and if there is a large number of flowering plants in them, feeding with a high potash fertilizer will encourage flowers.

EARLY AUTUMN

Make an outdoor mushroom bed: Most amateur gardeners who try their hand at growing mushrooms use the boxed kits that are widely available. These are kept indoors, and usually you can get five or six pickings from them. However, now is a good time to plant up an outdoor mushroom bed in a shady part of the garden, preferably under the protection of a wall and where the soil is consistently moist.

Feed lawns: Grass that is predominately in the shade should be given its second feed of the year, using a proprietary lawn fertilizer formulated for autumn use. Before you do this, however, it makes sense to put down a mosskiller to eradicate this problem if it is present (it is common on shaded lawns). Mosskiller products are widely available.

Pests and diseases: When and where it is necessary, continue spraying against pests and diseases until mid-autumn, after which chemical controls become ineffective – both the insect pests and the fungal problems will have gone past their active life cycles.

ABOVE Mid-autumn is the time to plant spring-flowering bulbs, including fritillaries seen here being planted between wallflowers.

ABOVE Clearing leaves from pathways, particularly shaded paths where the sun cannot dry them out, is important if you are to avoid dangerous and slippery conditions.

MID-AUTUMN

Planting: Woody plants ordered in mid-summer, or at other times, will probably be arriving now. As soon as they arrive, unpack them. If you are not able to plant them straight away, heel them in so that the roots do not dry out. Then, as soon as you are able, follow the planting procedures outlined on pages 30–39.

Bulbs: Shade-loving, spring-flowering bulbs such as crocus, bluebells and snowdrops, along with the many other bulbs should be planted now. Tulips and hyacinths, however, should be left until late autumn.

Check supports: Supports for trees, and climbing plants growing on trelliswork, should always be firm, but the action of autumn frosts and winds, or simple old age can cause them to be broken or otherwise unstable. Now is a good time to replace these where necessary. Also, check that ties are secure, but not too tight.

Sow lawns: Grass seed will germinate well enough at this time, but you could also wait until spring if this is more convenient. Choose a grass seed mixture that is recommended for shade, which will probably contain wood meadow grass (*Poa nemoralis*) and fine-leaved fescue (*Festuca tenuifolia*).

LATE AUTUMN

Tidy up borders: By this time most herbaceous plants will have lost most of their leaves and many will have died down to practically nothing. Cut off all remaining dead and dying stems and leaves (but make sure you leave the green leaves and stems of *Helleborus*).

Prepare the soil: New beds may be dug, and old ones renovated (see early winter).

Autumn leaves: Remove dead leaves from flowerbeds, rockeries, lawns and footpaths. If left to rot in place they will harm, or even kill, the growing plants or grass beneath them. On paths they can become slippery and dangerous. Burn leaves if there was a severe problem of mildew or rust during the previous growing season.

Check equipment: If secateurs and pruners are not cutting cleanly, sharpen the angled side of the blade on a fine carborundum or oil stone. Smear the blades with an oily rag, and put a drop of oil on pivots. If sprayers were put away uncleaned, rinse them with warm water containing a little detergent. Undo the spray nozzle and clean it thoroughly.

Hygiene: Continue to weed as necessary. Pinch out and dispose of pests and diseases.

TYPICAL PLANT HARDINESS ZONES FOR WESTERN EUROPE

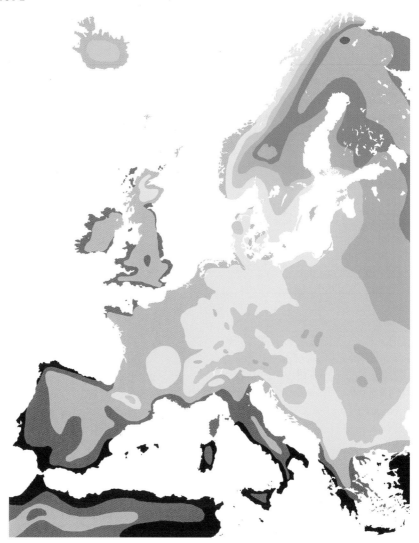

GROWING SHADE-LOVING PLANTS ACROSS THE WORLD

Conditions in Britain are similar to those found in some parts of Europe, so the same kinds of shade-loving plants should grow there quite happily. In areas such as the Mediterranean, adjustments may be needed, including extra watering. Factors including extremes of cold and hours of sunlight must also be taken into account.

Across North America, there are more extreme variations of temperature than those found across Britain and Northern Europe. To grow plants successfully, the factors that will need to be taken into consideration include the hours of cold weather in winter, how hot the summers are and whether the climate is damp or dry.

TYPICAL PLANT HARDINESS ZONES FOR NORTH AMERICA

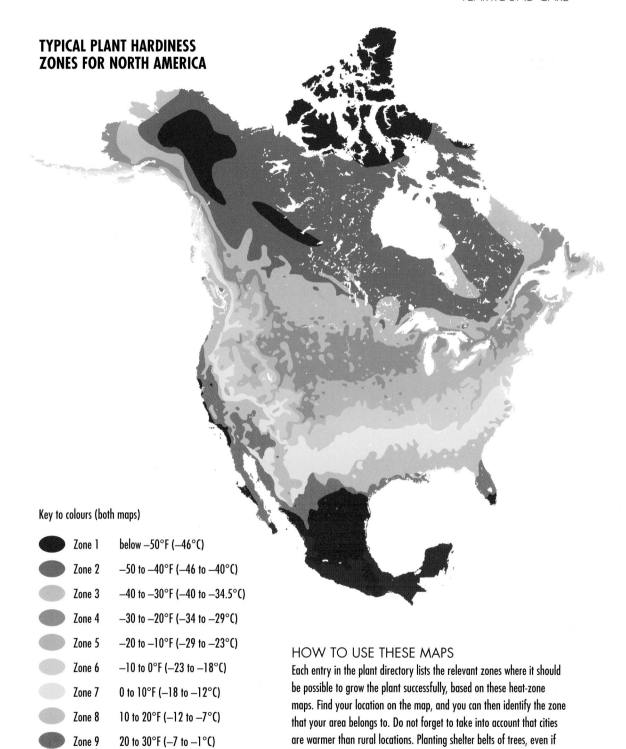

Key to colours (both maps)

	Zone 1	below −50°F (−46°C)
	Zone 2	−50 to −40°F (−46 to −40°C)
	Zone 3	−40 to −30°F (−40 to −34.5°C)
	Zone 4	−30 to −20°F (−34 to −29°C)
	Zone 5	−20 to −10°F (−29 to −23°C)
	Zone 6	−10 to 0°F (−23 to −18°C)
	Zone 7	0 to 10°F (−18 to −12°C)
	Zone 8	10 to 20°F (−12 to −7°C)
	Zone 9	20 to 30°F (−7 to −1°C)
	Zone 10	30 to 40°F (−1 to 4°C)
	Zone 11	above 40°F (above 4°C)

HOW TO USE THESE MAPS

Each entry in the plant directory lists the relevant zones where it should be possible to grow the plant successfully, based on these heat-zone maps. Find your location on the map, and you can then identify the zone that your area belongs to. Do not forget to take into account that cities are warmer than rural locations. Planting shelter belts of trees, even if these are in the shade and/or in raised, well-drained beds, can help to give plants better conditions in which to thrive.

SECTION TWO

LEFT **A shaded garden gives the chance
to grow a wide range of plants.**

71

CHAPTER 7

A–Z plant directory

This part of the book will be an invaluable source of reference when you are choosing plants to grow in your shady garden, or identifying plants you see and like. You'll be able to find the descriptions of more than 100 of our most popular garden plants, and see what many of them look like too. Plants are listed alphabetically within the section that relates to their type (annuals, bulbs, perennials, trees and shrubs and so on). Under each of the descriptions are these items of information:

Origin: This tells you, if known, where the species was discovered. Understanding where a plant comes from, the country or part of the world, with its average climate or even altitude, can help you to understand its growing requirements and conditions.

Type: The 'type' of plant – for example, whether it is grown from a bulb as opposed to a tuber, corm or rhizome, or whether it is an annual (grows, flowers and dies within one year) or a biennial (the same but in two years), or perhaps a shrub rather than a climber.

USDA zone: These are the climate zones referred to on pages 68–69, designed to identify the relative hardiness of plants. The zone numbers quoted here, based on UK Royal Horticultural Sociey data, are on the cautious side, so if you are not prepared to take any

chances, follow the hardiness ratings to the letter. Otherwise there is a great deal of leeway. Raised beds, good drainage, tree cover, east-facing as opposed to west-facing gardens, and planting against a house wall all give plants a better habitat – so be prepared to experiment.

Description: Here you will discover generalized details of the plant's shape, size and general demeanour, along with flower and foliage colour and shape.

Shade preference: Here there is an indication of whether the plant in question prefers light, dappled or dense shade conditions.

Popular species and varieties: Sometimes a plant species will exist without offspring or siblings. This will therefore have a relatively small entry in this book. But with, for example, the *Hosta* genus, there are hundreds of different species and cultivars (abbreviation of 'cultivated variety' – see below) and so there will be many to recommend.

HOW PLANTS ARE NAMED

If the name of the plant is all in italics, then this is a naturally occurring plant that has been discovered growing in its wild habitat, and been grown in number to be introduced to gardens. Take *Hosta ventricosa*, for example. *Hosta* is the genus name and *ventricosa* is the species name; this is a plant that was originally discovered growing wild in China, and therefore is a 'true' species.

Different plant hunters and botanists have over the years found slightly different forms or variations of recognized species, so sometimes you will see f. or var. or subsp. in the names of the plants. These describe naturally occurring forms (f.), varieties (var.) or subspecies (subsp.).

However, if you see a name such as *Hosta* 'Hadspen Blue', this tells you that the plant is a cultivar, and plant breeders and hybridizers have been selecting and crossing plants to produce and reproduce a distinctive plant that they can then name.

Therefore, if you see a plant name that has part of it within quote marks, as above, you will know that this is a cultivar (contraction of cultivated variety) and not a true species.

Syn. is an abbreviation for 'synonym', which refers to the fact that the plant is well known by, or may be sold under, an alternative name.

ANNUALS AND BIENNIALS

NAME: *AGERATUM* (FLOSSFLOWER)

Origin: Central and South America
Type: Annual
Shade preference: Dappled to light
USDA Zone: Not applicable (annuals grow and die within a single growing year, and so do not overwinter).
Description: Soft flowers in blue (mainly) but also pink or white, in compact, long-lasting clusters. One of the most popular of summer annuals for edging a bed or border.

Popular species and varieties: *Ageratum houstonianum* 'Blue Mink' is 9–12in (23–30cm) high, with powder-blue flowers that are carried until mid-autumn. 'Blue Swords' has flowers that are a distinct violet-blue, and 'Album' has pure white flowers.

ABOVE *Ageratum* 'Blue Swords'

NAME: *BEGONIA SEMPERFLORENS* (BEDDING OR WAX BEGONIA)

Origin: South America
Type: Tender perennial grown as an annual
Shade preference: Dappled
USDA Zone: Z9–11
Description: Often referred to as the fibrous-rooted begonias (because the other popular types emerge from bulb-like tubers), this group of hybrids and cultivars, usually about 8–12in (20–30cm) high, have bronze to green leaves. Flowers of white, pink or red, up to 1in (2.5cm) across, bloom continuously outdoors in summer. Many varieties have single or double blossoms, some quite large, whilst others have numerous clusters of small flowers.

Popular species and varieties: An excellent foil for many summer bedding plants, the cultivar 'Gin' has attractive bronze leaves and white flowers with yellow stamens. 'Stara Mixed' has large flowers and 'Two Tones' comprises a mixture of bicolours each with dark bronze and green foliage – the 'two tone' effect.

ABOVE *Campanula medium*

NAME: *CAMPANULA MEDIUM* (CANTERBURY BELLS)

Origin: South-eastern Europe, Mediterranean
Type: Biennial
Shade preference: Dappled to light
USDA Zone: Z6–10
Description: Canterbury bells comprise an important group of biennials that come in a range of violet-blue shades. Plants are some 2–4ft (60–120cm) high; flowers are solitary, or in loose clusters on the stalks, and are frequently 1in (2.5cm) wide and 2in (5cm) long.

Popular species and varieties: The usual forms are straight *C. medium*, sometimes sold as 'Canterbury Bells Mixed', available in a wide range of blues, whites and pink. 'Dwarf Double Melton Bells Mixed' reaches a height of 36in (90cm), and has flowers so double that the petals obscure the centre of the bell. Large, wax-like blooms smother the plant in a delightful cerise-pink, rose-pink and deep glossy blue.

ABOVE *Begonia semperflorens* 'Stara Mixed'

ABOVE *Cleome* 'Pink Queen'

ABOVE *Cosmos* 'Sensation Mixed'

NAME: *CLEOME* (SPIDER FLOWER)

Origin: Tropical America
Type: Annual
Shade preference: Dappled to light
USDA Zone: Not applicable (annuals grow and die within a single growing year, and so do not overwinter).
Description: This annual, which reaches a height of 4–5ft (1.2–1.5m) is bushy, and lends an airy, tropical feel to beds and mixed borders, naturalizing schemes and the rough, half-cultivated areas of a large garden. The finger-like leaves are sticky, with 3–7 leaflets. The blooms are rose-purple, pink, or white clustered in loose, spidery wheels at the tops of the stems.
Popular species and varieties: The main form, *Cleome spinosa*, is usually available, but the form 'Colour Fountain Mixed' has a slightly wider colour range which, in addition to the above shades, also includes lilac; 'Pink Queen' carries large flowers of clear sugar-pink.

NAME: *COSMOS BIPINNATUS*

Origin: Central America, Mexico
Type: Annual
Shade preference: Dappled to light
USDA Zone: Not applicable (annuals grow and die within a single growing year, and so do not overwinter).
Description: Plant this showy summer and early autumn-flowering annual at the mid-point or back of the border, or in large massed plantings. Plants can grow up to 8ft (2.5m), but usually reach 3–4ft (1–1.2m). The habit is open, and branching, and the foliage is bright green and lacy. The daisy-like flowers are 3–6in (7.5–15cm) wide, and are single, double or crested. They have white, pink, crimson or lavender petals, often notched or frilled, with yellow centres. Excellent as a cut flower.
Popular species and varieties: 'Candy Stripe' has ice-white blooms, boldly bordered, splashed or stippled with crimson (occasionally a pure crimson bloom may appear); 'Daydream' has smaller flowers than most, and they are freely produced; 'Pied Piper Red' has fluted shell-like petals of velvet crimson-red; 'Sensation Mixed' comprises a large selection of shades in whites, pinks and carmine-reds.

ABOVE *Dianthus barbatus* 'Roundabout'

ABOVE *Digitalis purpurea*

NAME: *DIANTHUS BARBATUS* (SWEET WILLIAM)

Origin: Throughout Europe, Asia and the eastern US

Type: Biennial

Shade preference: Dappled to light

USDA Zone: Z5–8

Description: The old-fashioned Sweet William is excellent as a cut flower, summer bedder and filler in immature beds and borders. Compact varieties make a cheerful edging to rock gardens. Reaching 1–2ft (30–60cm) in height, the numerous red, rose-purple, white or variously coloured blooms are fragrant. Sometimes the blooms are double.

Popular species and varieties: There are masses of named cultivars, and mixtures available to grow from seed. They include: 'Excelsior Mixed' (strongly scented); 'Indian Carpet Mixed' and 'Nanus' (dwarf at just 6in (15cm) high), 'Noverna' (in shades of red, pink and purple) and 'Roundabout' (red-centred flowers in shades of magenta, rose-pink, carmine and white).

NAME: *DIGITALIS* (FOXGLOVE)

Origin: Europe, north-west Africa, central Asia

Type: Biennial

Shade preference: Dappled

USDA Zone: Z6–8

Description: The foxglove is one of the western world's most familiar wild woodland plants. Its spikes of nodding bell-shaped blooms appear from late spring to mid-summer. From these flowers the seeds drop and quickly germinate to form new plants that overwinter and come to flowering prominence the following summer, when the exercise is repeated. Slightly fuzzy leaves are coarse and medium green, forming a basal rosette. All parts of the plant are poisonous (containing digitalin, which affects the functioning of the heart – for which, curiously, it is still used today in some medicines for heart conditions).

Popular species and varieties: 'Alba', 'Apricot' or 'Excelsior Hybrid Mixed', are all 4–5ft (1.2–1.5m) tall, and all bred from the common, foxglove (*Digitalis purpurea*); *D. x mertonensis* grows to 30in (75cm); *D. grandiflora* grows to 36in (90cm).

ABOVE *Impatiens* 'Fiesta Sparkling Rose'

NAME: *IMPATIENS* (BUSY LIZZIE)

Origin: Globally, except South America, Australia and New Zealand
Type: Tender perennial, designed to be grown as an annual
Shade preference: Light
USDA Zone: 10
Description: Low-growing highly floriferous bedding plants for summer. They come in a variety of colours from white and pale pink through to oranges, deep reds and near purple. Yellow and blue shades have yet to be bred. All flower from early summer until the autumn frosts.
Popular species and varieties: 'Super Elfin' series of F1 hybrids, to 10in (25cm), available in individual colours, such as 'Lipstick' (rose-pink), 'Salmon Blush' (peachy salmon) and 'Velvet Red' (deep red); or 'Fiesta Sparkling Rose', or a mixture, as in 'Bruno' F1 hybrid, with large flowers up to 2.5in (6cm) across, growing to 9in (23cm). The 'Accent Bright Eye' series has flowers of more than 2in (5cm) across. The Spellbound range of *Impatiens*, including 'Cranberry Cauldron' and 'Fairy Pink', are particularly free-flowering.

NAME: LOBELIA (EDGING, ANNUAL OR TRAILING LOBELIA)

Origin: North America
Type: Annual
Shade preference: Light
USDA Zone: Not applicable (annuals grow and die within a single growing year, and so do not overwinter).
Description: Bedding lobelias (as opposed to the perennial red *Lobelia cardinalis*) are grown for their low-growing blue, purple, crimson and white flowers. It is a great favourite for borders, although it is demanding in its habits, needing a humus-rich soil if it is to thrive. Many of the new *Lobelia* hybrids seek to vary the length of the stems and to extend the colour range. It can be planted to trail from a hanging basket or tumble over a patio container.
Popular species and varieties: 'Cambridge Blue' (mid-blue) and 'Mrs Clibran Improved' (deep blue with a white eye) both grow to 4in (10cm) in height; 'Cascade' is an excellent trailing variety in a wide colour range.

ABOVE *Lobelia* 'Mrs Clibran Improved'

ABOVE *Lunaria annua 'Variegata'*

like seedpods. It is chiefly grown for the pods, which are excellent in dried arrangements. This fragrant, if somewhat weedy plant, likes dappled to light shade, and the deeper the shade the better, if you live in a hot part of the world. It is a good candidate for naturalizing in a shady part of the garden.

Popular species and varieties: Seed of the straight species (with pink flowers), or its several named forms, is surprisingly difficult to find; however, it is worth the search. 'Alba' has white flowers, and there is also a form ('Variegata') with variegated leaves, and another with purplish foliage.

NAME: *LUNARIA ANNUA* (HONESTY)

Origin: Southern Europe
Type: Biennial
Shade preference: Dappled to light
USDA Zone: Z6–8
Description: The bright purple or white summer flowers of this familiar biennial are followed by the characteristic round, flattened, parchment-

NAME: *MIMULUS CUPREUS* (MONKEY FLOWER)

Origin: Chile
Type: Perennial, but treated as an annual
Shade preference: Light
USDA Zone: Typically Z7–10
Description: These plants are rather short-lived and thrive in wet soils, making a bright show of colour in summer with their tubular blooms of

ABOVE *Mimulus 'Big Boy'*

velvety petals spotted at the flower throat. They come in a range of reds, oranges, yellows and bicolours. The parent species grows in Chilean bogs, and the hybrids retain a trace of this characteristic for they prefer moist areas. However, they are versatile enough to be successfully grown in windowboxes or small gardens on the shady side of a building.

Popular species and varieties: *Mimulus cupreus* has bronzy-orange, brown-spotted flowers, with a height and spread of 12in (30cm). *M. cardinalis* (red and yellow flowers) grows to a height of 24in (60cm), and a spread of 12in (30cm); *M. luteus* (yellow, crimson-spotted) has a variable height from 6–24in (15–60cm), and has a spread of some 12in (30cm); the hybrid 'Big Boy' has particularly large flowers that are vividly coloured.

NAME: *MYOSOTIS SYLVATICA* (FORGET-ME-NOT)

Origin: Throughout Europe and parts of Asia
Type: Biennial
Shade preference: Dappled to dense
USDA Zone: Z4–8
Description: These are low-growing, moisture-loving plants prized for their small but numerous, usually blue flowers. In the self-sown forms there will be some flowers with a central white eye, and others with a yellow eye. Forget-me-nots prefer a moist soil, cool weather and, curiously, they like crowded conditions where they can support each other in a border. They are particularly good as a planting beneath and between tall bulbs.

Popular species and varieties: 'Blue Ball' produces compact, ball-shaped plants just 6in (15cm) tall, with flowers of bright blue; 'Bobo Mixed' are normally blue, but pink and white flowers also appear on different plants; 'Royal Blue Improved' is taller, at 12in (30cm), and has deep indigo-blue flowers.

RIGHT *Myosotis sylvatica*

ABOVE *Nemophila menziesii*

ABOVE *Nicotiana* 'Tinkerbell'

NAME: *NEMOPHILA MENZIESII* (BABY BLUE EYES)

Origin: North America
Type: Annual
Shade preference: Light
USDA Zone: Not applicable (annuals grow and die within a single growing year, and so do not overwinter).
Description: The flowers of these annuals are in showy clusters, and appear from early summer to early autumn; the leaves are usually deeply divided. These are cool-weather flowers that do well in cooler gardens or those at high altitudes. They grow quickly and easily, preferring afternoon shade. *Nemophila* is usually best used as a ground cover under taller bulbs or shrubs, or for naturalizing.

Popular species and varieties: *Nemophila menziesii* is a trailing plant growing to 12in (30cm). The bright blue flowers are bell-shaped, and there are white, and blue and white forms. *N. maculata* 'Pennie Black' (purple with white edge) grows to 4in (10cm); *N. maculata* 'Five Spot' (white with blue-tipped petals) grows to 3–6in (8–15cm); *N. maculata* 'Chelsea Blue' (lilac-blue with deep lilac-tipped petals).

NAME: *NICOTIANA ALATA* (FLOWERING TOBACCO PLANT)

Origin: South America
Type: Annual or short-lived perennial
Shade preference: Dappled to light
USDA Zone: Z7
Description: Popular garden plants for their showy, long-blooming flowers which first open at night. The sap has narcotic, and poisonous,

properties, which is hardly surprising when you come to realize that tobacco is derived from the close relative, *Nicotiana tabacum*. The garden annuals can reach 5ft (1.5m) in height, with branching stems. The blooms are frequently fragrant, and are shaped like small trumpets or funnels. Colours are numerous, including white, pink, mauve, maroon, purple and even green.

Popular species and varieties: Many varieties are available, some with larger flowers, and some day-blooming dwarf kinds with showier but less fragrant blossoms. 'Domino Antique Shades' is a hybrid strain with a compact habit just 12in (30cm) high, making it perfect for pots and border edges; 'Tinkerbell', at 36in (90cm) high, has dusky rose-pink flowers with blue pollen and contrasting lime-green backs. *Nicotiana knightiana* 'Green Tears' is smothered in small, two-toned green, teardrop-like blooms; *Nicotiana sylvestris* produces a candelabra of highly fragrant white blooms – a choice plant for the border, or as a 'dot' plant amongst other bedding, and a real talking point.

NAME: *SOLENOSTEMON* (COLEUS, OR FLAME NETTLE)

Origin: Tropical Africa and Asia
Type: Short-lived perennial, grown as an annual
Shade preference: Dappled to dense
USDA Zone: Z10
Description: These provide brightly coloured leaves for beds and containers, and fillers in flower arrangements. They make very good projects for children to grow. Most forms will grow to a height of some 3ft (90cm) if potted on and fed. They have square stems, characteristic of members of the Labiatae plant family (which also includes nettles, sage and lavender). The leaves are variously edged with serrations, or fringed, but it is the multitudes of colours that make these plants popular. Common colours include greens, creams, pinks, reds, oranges and maroon combinations.

Popular species and varieties: Mixtures are available, with no particular varietal names, which adds to the fun when growing as you do not know what you are getting! Varieties to look for, however, include 'Wizard Scarlet' (rich, vibrant velvet-red edged in bright gold); 'Wizard Sunset' (apricot leaves with a hint of a yellow edge); 'Pallisandra' (very large purple, almost black leaves that provide a foil to other plants); 'Tilt-a-Whirl' (flame orange and pale green on curved leaves). Particularly good is 'Kong Mixed', a recent breeding breakthrough, with enormous, eye-catching leaves up to 12in (30cm) long in a mixture of colours.

ABOVE *Solenostemon scutellaroides* 'Tilt-a-Whirl'

FLOWERING BULBOUS PLANTS

This part of the Directory looks at 'bulbous' plants, but in fact most of the subjects covered could grow from bulbs, corms, tubers or, in some cases, rhizomes. Before we examine them in detail, let's clear up some of the confusion that surrounds these groups.

Bulbs are essentially fleshy modified leaves enclosing an embryonic flower – which means that when you buy a bulb you can almost guarantee that it will flower. Popular examples are *Hyacinthus*, *Tulipa* and *Narcissus*.

Tubers and corms are also often described as 'bulbs', and this causes confusion with gardeners. All three types are basic storage organs for the plant, containing a supply of water and food that keeps the plant alive while it is dormant; however, most tubers and corms are also modified, swollen stems. New shoots emanate from buds at the tops of the organs. *Anemone* and *Cyclamen* are good examples of tuberous plants for a shady garden, *Crocus* is an example of a corm.

A rhizome is a fleshy underground stem that acts as a storage organ, and perhaps the best examples here are *Eranthis* and *Trillium*. Each year the rhizome produces buds and shoots from the end, so the older part dies and shrivels. The term 'rhizome' is also used sometimes to refer to over-ground shoots that then root some distance from the parent plant. The pernicious weed couch grass, or twitch, is the most obvious example.

NAME: *ANEMONE* (WINDFLOWER)

Origin: North America, Europe, Asia
Type: Rhizomatous and tuberous perennials
Shade preference: Dappled to light
USDA Zone: Z4–8
Description: There are a great many species and cultivars of *Anemone*, ranging from 6in (15cm) to 4ft (1.2m) in height, and flowering variously from early spring to late autumn. Many are woodland plants, the common name deriving from the way the flowerheads nod in the breeze.
Popular species and varieties: *Anemone blanda* AGM grows from tubers, and is available in shades of white, pink and blue-purple. It has open daisy-like flowers, the first of which, in mild seasons, can appear even in mid-winter, but it is normally at its best in early spring. It reaches just 6in (15cm) in height. Garden centres usually sell these plants in mixed pots or packets, but occasionally you will find named varieties. Those to look out for include: 'Radar' AGM – the oldest and the best – which is a bright magenta daisy-like bloom with a white centre; 'White Splendour', has large, pure white flowers; 'Charmer', is a clear pink and 'Atrocaerulea' is pale blue. Also growing from tubers, *Anemone coronaria* is very popular, mainly in the form of two strains descended from this species – the De Caen Group (often known as the Poppy Anemone) and St Brigid Group. Colours range from deep blue and purple shades, through to red, pink and white. The St Brigids come in semi- or double-flowering forms. As with the forms of *A. blanda*, tubers are usually sold in mixes; however, several named varieties are available, including 'The Bride' (single, white), the dramatic 'Hollandia' (scarlet, single) and the intense 'Lord Lieutenant' (deep blue, double). All of these are good as cut flowers. The two final recommendations grow from underground rhizomes: the white wood anemone (*A. nemorosa* AGM) is ideal for naturalizing under trees and shrubs; *A. ranunculoides* produces lovely buttercup-yellow blooms in early spring.

ABOVE *Anemone blanda* 'Atrocaerulea'

NAME: *ARUM MARMORATUM* (LORDS AND LADIES)

Origin: Throughout Europe and Asia
Type: Tuberous perennials
Shade preference: Dappled to dense
USDA Zone: Z6–7
Description: Although the white-flowering *Zantedeschia aethiopeca* is known as the arum lily, it is actually a misnomer, as the true arums are members of the *Arum* genus, such as *A. italicum* and *A. marmoratum* (often known as cuckoo pint, or lords and ladies). This latter plant is particularly useful for a woodland garden, producing much needed fresh and bright foliage in the depths of winter. These marbled leaves are often used by flower arrangers, as indeed are the fruiting spikes comprizing thick clusters of bright orange-red berries. Attractive though they are, the berries are poisonous. The flowers are typical of the *Arum* family in that they comprise a flat, spade-like structure, called a 'spathe'.
Popular species and varieties: The best form of *A. italicum* is often referred to as 'Pictum' but its accepted botanical name now is *A. italicum* subsp. *italicum* 'Marmoratum'. The hybrid 'Chameleon' produces large, more rounded leaves with greyish markings on them, whilst 'White Winter' should be grown for its dramatic silver foliage. The yellow spathed *A. creticum* can sometimes be found in other colour forms. *A. concinnatum* produces a flower of dull yellow, or often creamy purple!

ABOVE *Arum italicum*

NAME: *CARDIOCRINUM GIGANTEUM* AGM (GIANT LILY)

Origin: The Himalayas, through China to Japan

Type: Bulbous and monocarpic (dying after flowering, usually leaving behind one or two offsets that take two or three years to reach flowering size).

Shade preference: Dappled to light

USDA Zone: Z7

Description: 'Dramatic' hardly does these gigantic flowers justice. Related to lilies, they make a talking point for anyone who sees them. *Cardiocrinum giganteum* AGM is the only species generally available and can, in ideal conditions, grow to 8ft (2.5m) and produce a magnificent display of scented, trumpet-shaped blooms. They are white with a purplish tinge on the inside and a green flush on the outside. The foliage is very different to that of other lilies, in that individual leaves are broad and glossy, and held at the base of the stem. They can be up to 18in (45cm) across, reducing in size up the stem. It is a good idea to plant bulbs of different sizes as this should ensure that you have some in bloom most years.

Popular species and varieties: Usually only this species is available.

ABOVE *Cardiocrinum giganteum* AGM

84

ABOVE *Colchicum speciosum* 'Atrorubens'

NAME: *COLCHICUM AUTUMNALE* (AUTUMN CROCUS)

Origin: Central and Western Europe
Type: Perennial corm
Shade preference: Dappled to light
USDA Zone: Z5
Description: These very colourful autumn flowers grow from corms. Because of their crocus-like flowers they are, confusingly, referred to as 'autumn crocus', but in fact they are not related to each other at all. These plants make a wonderful autumnal 'surprise' when their flower buds emerge from the soil. The leaves follow in the late winter. When in full leaf colchicums are large, and could be thought of as plant 'thugs' – they have been known to smother smaller plants. Two words of warning: they are poisonous, and they can look unsightly in a border when dying back, so you are advised to choose their position with care.

Popular species and varieties: The best known is *Colchicum autumnale*, which produces masses of lilac-pink goblet-shaped flowers – and all from a single corm. It is a good plant for naturalizing in grass. 'Alboplenum' is white, double and produces three to five flowers from each bulb. 'The Giant' has rose-lilac flowers on 10in (25cm) long stalks; each flower has a white base. If you prefer something a little less showy, there is the single, white cultivar: 'Album'. *C. speciosum* 'Atrorubens' is a vivid sugar pink, whilst 'Waterlily' AGM has purplish-lilac double flowers (in many ways this last variety really does resemble a bloom of the waterlily).

NAME: *CYCLAMEN*

Origin: Southern Europe and the Mediterranean
Type: Tuberous perennials
Shade preference: Dappled to light
USDA Zone: Z6–9
Description: Cyclamen are best known as winter-flowering pot plants for bringing into cool rooms indoors, and into conservatories. The hardy forms, however, make graceful and extremely useful plants for growing in shady spots under trees. They are most dramatic when grown en masse, and in time they will grow into large colonies of colour.
Popular species and varieties: *C. hederifolium* AGM comes into bloom in late summer. It is a curiosity that the first flowers often appear just after rainfall. Blooms appear before the leaves. There are both pink and white forms. A great attraction of the plant is the varied shapes and patterning of the leaves – none are the same, marbling, blotches and silvering all commonplace. Late winter will see the *Cyclamen coum* AGM in all its glory, seemingly quite unaffected by cold weather – in some years it will bloom in early winter, but this cannot be guaranteed. The pointed buds open to pink or white. Most have rounded leaves with lovely silver and green patterning in the top, and plain dark red on the underside. Although the plants themselves are tough, the leaves can be damaged by a severe frost.

Other *Cyclamen* suited to a lightly shaded part of the garden include *C. libanoticum* AGM (large clear pink flowers in spring), *C. cilicium* AGM (pink in autumn), *C. cilicium* f. *album* (white in autumn) and *C. graecum*, the pink flowers of which are held well clear of heavily marbled foliage. Finally, *C. repandum* has beautifully reddish-purple turned-back petals in spring.

ABOVE *Cyclamen hederifolium* 'Album'

NAME: *ERANTHIS HYEMALIS* AGM (WINTER ACONITE)

Origin: Southern Europe
Type: Rhizomatous perennial
Shade preference: Dappled
USDA Zone: Z5
Description: The buttercup-yellow aconites are a really cheery sight in late winter. The cup-shaped flowers, supported by collars of green, deeply toothed bracts, distinguish these from other winter plants such as hellebores and snowdrops; they are like nothing else, and every garden should try to make room for one or two of them

Popular species and varieties: The winter aconite (*Eranthis hyemalis* AGM) will seed itself if the conditions are right, and will in time form a large carpet of late winter colour. *Eranthis* x *tubergenii* has larger blooms, and the form 'Guinea Gold' AGM is particularly vigorous.

ABOVE *Eranthis hyemalis* 'Guinea Gold' AGM

NAME: *ERYTHRONIUM*

Origin: Europe, Asia, northern United States
Type: Tuberous perennials
Shade preference: Dappled
USDA Zone: Z3–5
Description: The delicate-looking erythroniums are tough woodland plants that are suitable for growing under deciduous trees, or on a lightly shaded rock garden. Their spring flowers are dainty, in both stature and colour.
Popular species and varieties: The easy-to-grow *Erythronium dens-canis* AGM has the rather curious common name of dogs-tooth violet, which originates from the shape of the fleshy pointed bulb that loosely resembles a dog's tooth. Its blooms are pink-purple and are carried well above the mottled green and brown leaves. There are a number of named cultivars, among them 'Catheum', with flesh-pink blooms, and 'Album', white.

'Pagoda' AGM is vigorous plant, and in ideal conditions will naturalize itself. The flowers, which are somewhat larger, are yellow, and four or five may be carried on a single 12in (30cm) stem. Slightly paler yellow are the flower of the hybrid 'Kondo'.

The American trout lily (*E. revolutum* AGM) carries pink lantern flowers with prominent yellow anthers on strong 12in (30cm) high stems, held well clear of the brown-purple mottled foliage. *E. tuolumnense* has bright yellow flowers with distinctive green veining. *E. californicum* AGM has mid-green foliage that is lightly mottled silvery green. The cream-white flowers with their reflexed petals are held on stems 8in (20cm) high. Look particularly for the pure white 'White Beauty' AGM. Its blooms have soft yellow anthers that contrast well against brown-centred leaves.

NAME: *FRITILLARIA*
(FRITILLARIES, OR CROWN IMPERIALS)

Origin: Throughout the northern hemisphere
Type: Bulbous perennials
Shade preference: Light
USDA Zone: Z4–5
Description: The true crown imperial (*Fritillaria imperialis*) is most eye-catching with its sturdy stems and deep orange bell-shaped flowers – but it does have a somewhat unpleasant fox-like odour when examined at close quarters. However, do not let this put you off. It is a native of the Himalayas and grows to around 36in (90cm) in height. The glossy leaves are produced up the dark brown stems to about half way. The remaining parts of the stem are bare, until you come to the orange blooms grouped in

ABOVE *Erythronium 'Kondo'*

ABOVE *Fritillaria imperialis*

a cluster. These are topped by a crown of pointed green leaves; altogether a most curious looking plant.

Popular species and varieties: Cultivars include 'The Premier' (soft tangerine-orange) and 'Maxima Lutea' AGM (golden-yellow). Much smaller, the purple chequered flowers of the snake's head fritillary, *F. meleagris* AGM, which always attract attention. The bell-shaped pendant flowers are carried in pairs on thin stems 8in (20cm) high. 'Aphrodite' is a pure white form. *F. persica* 'Adiyaman' AGM has dark plum-purple bell flowers along most of its 24in (60cm) stems; it is a vigorous plant with leaves of plain green.

In mid-spring my bulb display is enhanced by a small clump of *F. uva-vulpis* growing under an apple tree in a border. One of the daintier fritillaries, the small bulbs put up stems over 12in (30cm) long, each topped by a lone flower whose brownish-pink petals are tipped with yellow. They come up every year without fail.

ABOVE *Galanthus elwesii AGM*

NAME: *GALANTHUS* (SNOWDROP)

Origin: Western Europe
Type: Bulbous perennial
Shade preference: Dappled to dense
USDA Zone: Z4–6
Description: With their nodding white flowers, snowdrops are one of our favourite winter-flowering bulbs. There are many species and cultivars, yet to the untrained eye they all look very similar. They have a large, almost cult following, with enthusiasts studying the minutia of flower shape, colour, markings and so on.

Popular species and varieties: The common snowdrop (*Galanthus nivalis* AGM) is the most widely grown form. It grows from 4–8in (10–20cm) high, and produces its finest show in a fertile soil in partial shade. The blue-grey leaves are flat and strap-shaped; the white flowers have small green markings on the central sets of petals. 'Flore Pleno' AGM is a double form, and among the named varieties look for 'S. Arnott' AGM which is slightly scented, and 'Viridapicis' with a green spot on both the inner and outer petals. 'Lady Elphinstone' has attractive yellow markings.

G. *elwesii* AGM is often called the giant snowdrop. Its broad, grey-blue leaves accompany the large flowers on 10in (25cm) high stems. The blooms have three long petals, and three shorter ones with bright green markings. G. *elwesii* var. *monostictus* is one of the earliest to flower, in late autumn.

G. *ikariae* flowers in early spring; the wide foliage is bright glossy green. This is a distinctive variety with long outer petals, the shorter inner ones have typical green markings. 'Straffan' is an old favourite with large blooms on 6in (15cm) high stems, whilst 'Magnet' AGM has heavy flowers that nod and move in even the slightest of winds.

ABOVE *Hyacinthoides hispanica*

NAME: *HYACINTHOIDES* (BLUEBELL)

Origin: Western Europe
Type: Bulbous perennial
Shade preference: Light to deep
USDA Zone: Z5
Description: Bluebells are woodland plants, and herald the arrival of spring, flowering before the trees above them come into full leaf.
Popular species and varieties: The vigorous rich blue Spanish bluebell, *Hyacinthoides hispanica* used to be known as *Scilla campanulata* and you may still occasionally see it sold under this name. It is a good plant for growing in groups in the border. Large bell-shaped blooms are carried on stems 12in (30cm) high from mid- to late spring. They are often sold in colour mixtures, but are arguably better when planted in groups of the same colour. 'Queen of the Pinks' is a delicate rose-pink; 'White City' has flowers of pure white.

The English bluebell (*H. non-scripta*) can be identified by its deep blue colouring and smaller, daintier, more widely spaced blooms. The flower stem has a delicate appearance, curving over slightly at the top. Each bloom hangs down from the stem like a little bell, its petals curling back on themselves at the tips to reveal creamy yellow anthers. If you do not want bluebells popping up all over your garden, deadhead them after flowering to prevent self-seeding.

NAME: *LEUCOJUM* (SNOWFLAKE)

Origin: Western Europe, North Africa
Type: Bulbous perennial
Shade preference: Light
USDA Zone: Z–5
Description: Pretty, white, bell-shaped flowers, usually tipped with green, are the feature of *Leucojum vernum* AGM, known as the spring snowflake. The eye-catching blooms are held on stems 4–8in (10–20cm) high. The glossy leaves are mid-green and strap-shaped, fairly short when the plants are in flower but growing longer as the season progresses. These are best planted in a place where the soil never really dries out in summer.

Popular species and varieties: *L. vernum* var. *carpathicum* is a spring snowflake with pale yellow spots at the tips of the petals. There are two other types of snowflake: the summer and autumn snowflakes. Confusingly, the former (*Leucojum aestivum*) normally flowers in late spring. This is a tall, more robust plant that can, in ideal conditions, reach 36in (90cm) in height; the stems carry white bell-shaped flowers tipped with green. The form 'Gravetye Giant' AGM has larger flowers and is a more vigorous plant. The autumn snowflake (*Leucojum autumnale* AGM) has thin stems carrying up to four small, white nodding bell-shaped flowers. It is a neat species reaching just 6in (15cm) or so in height, with narrow leaves.

ABOVE *Leucojum vernum* var. *carpathicum*

NAME: *LILIUM* (LILY)

Origin: Throughout the temperate regions of the northern hemisphere
Type: Bulbous perennials
Shade preference: Dappled to deep
USDA Zone: Z4–7
Description: Lilies have soared in popularity in recent years and now a garden would be considered by many to be incomplete without a few of these bulbs dotted about. They are quite happy in the ground provided they are not too exposed, are not in full sun and have a soil that is constantly moist but never waterlogged. They also make perfect plants for large pots, for bringing into full view when they are in flower.

The huge lily family consists of several groups and subdivisions, with flowers in many different forms from outward facing to trumpet-shaped, flattish blooms, and some referred to as Turk's cap lilies, with nodding, downward-facing flowers. Many species of *Lilium* are fragrant, so these should be positioned near to the house, patio or pathway, where they can be enjoyed at close quarters.

Popular species and varieties: *Lilium martagon*, known as the Turk's cap or Martagon lily, grows to 5ft (1.5m). Its flowers are rose-purple with dark spots; the petals are folded back. It is a very hardy species, and is good for naturalizing among shrubs or in grassy areas. It has been a parent to numerous hybrids, including a stunning white form, 'Album' AGM.

The Madonna lily (*Lilium candidum* AGM) produces strong 4ft (1.2m) high stems and carries fragrant pure white funnel-shaped flowers in early summer. These can be up to 6in (15cm) wide. This lily requires a warm, sheltered position. It is basal rooting, and can sometimes be difficult to establish; once planted, do not disturb it. The tiger lily (*L. lancifolium*) used to be called *L. tigrinum*; it has dark orange flowers with black spots to the petals, carried on stems 2–5ft (60cm–150cm) high. The golden-rayed lily, *L. auratum*, is a native of Japan; it has white,

ABOVE *Lilium regale AGM*

fragrant, saucer shaped flowers, each petal of which has a distinct yellow band running along its length. This is a lime-hating species, and is perhaps best grown in a container. Look out also for *L. auratum* var. *platyphyllum* AGM, with large waxy white flowers.

Many more splendid species lilies are available, and it is best to contact a specialist before making your choice.

There are hundreds of hybrid lilies, and some of the most dramatic are in the group known as the Orientals. These boast some excellent fragrant varieties among their number, all flowering from mid-summer onwards. They are lime-haters, so if your soil is alkaline grow them in containers. Among the best are 'Arena', large white flowers with a yellow star in the centre, and 'Casa Blanco' AGM, white with blooms 8in (20cm) across. 'Stargazer' is a rich crimson edged with white and spotted with maroon.

The Asiatic hybrids are easy to grow, producing sturdy growth with stems some 36–48in (90–120cm) high, and upward-facing blooms. Flowering takes place from early to mid-summer. Look for: 'Grand Cru', deep yellow, each petal marked with deep red; 'Lollipop', a cream-white with petal tips of deep pink; 'Enchantment' with bright orange-red blooms; 'Montreux', deep pink with light spots towards the centre; and 'Mont Blanc' with upward-facing flowers of cream-white. Trumpet lilies have stout stems and large trumpet-shaped flowers. Most bloom in mid-summer. The rich orange flower buds of 'African Queen' open to glossy orange trumpets; 'Golden Splendour' is deep yellow, its huge flowers held on 5ft (1.5m) stems.

The regal lily (*L. regale* AGM) is one of the best white funnel-shaped lilies. Its fragrant blooms in mid-summer can be 6in (15cm) long, with several on a stout stem. It does best in full sun, but nevertheless gives a very good account of itself in dappled shade. Finally, there is *L. longiflorum* – one of the most perfect of white lilies; often called the Easter lily it is best suited to growing in a pot. More than that, it does not like windy situations, so is really best in a conservatory that receives shade for a part of the day; it is also highly scented.

ABOVE *Ornithogalum umbellatum*

NAME: *ORNITHOGALUM* (STAR OF BETHLEHEM)

Origin: Mediterranean, South Africa
Type: Bulbous perennials
Shade preference: Dappled
USDA Zone: Z5–9

Description: The common name of Star of Bethlehem is appropriate, as *Ornithogalum* produces star-shaped flowers, and originates in the eastern fringes of Southern Europe. It is also widely seen throughout South Africa. For most of the year in our gardens it lies forgotten, until mid-spring when its whitish flower heads appear.

Popular species and varieties: *Ornithogalum umbellatum* is the most widely grown form. It is hardy and free-flowering, its glistening white flowers held over grass-like leaves. Good for naturalizing under trees, *O. nutans* AGM carries flowers of white and green and these are larger than *O. umbellatum*, are bell-shaped and nod in the breeze; they are held on 6–10in (15–25cm) high stems.

NAME: *SCILLA* (SQUILL)

Origin: USSR, Iran
Type: Bulbous perennials
Shade preference: Dappled to light
USDA Zone: Z5–6

Description: These plants can produce a veritable carpet of pale blue, dark blue and near white between mid-winter and mid-spring. *Scilla mischtschenkoana* can often be flowering at the same time as snowdrops. The best-known family member – *S. siberica* AGM – follows it, with lovely blue, nodding flowers.

Popular species and varieties: *Scilla sibirica* AGM is the loveliest and easiest species, and has over the years performed very well for me in light shade. Its leaves appear in early spring and are soon followed by the 4in (10cm) stems carrying three or four blue, bell- shaped flowers. *S. sibirica* 'Spring Beauty' is a robust form with larger bright blue flowers. 'Alba' is a good white-flowering variety.

The dainty *S. bifolia* AGM produces two strap-shaped leaves, which open out to allow a 4in (10cm) high stem, holding blue star-shaped flowers, in late winter. 'Rosea' is a purple-pink form and 'Alba' is white.

Scilla mischtschenkoana has pale blue flowers with a deeper blue stripe on each petal. It grows to 6in (15cm) in height and, like so many bulbs, is best planted in groups. Finally, *S. verna* has electric-blue flowers in spring.

NAME: *TRILLIUM* (WOOD LILY)

Origin: North-eastern Asia, Himalayas, North America
Type: Rhizomatous perennials
Shade preference: Dappled to deep
USDA Zone: Z4–6
Description: The name 'wood lily' does the *Trillium* a disservice. These are fabulous plants that can carpet a dappled glade with colour in spring. My personal favourites are the whites, but there are also purples, creams and greenish-yellows. As the genus name suggests, the blooms are made up of three petals. They are all bent backwards slightly, and are carried on stems 12in (30cm) or so high.
Popular species and varieties: Wake robin or *Trillium grandiflorum* AGM, is the most widely grown species. It is best in shady spots beneath deciduous trees. The double form 'Flore Pleno' AGM is a very desirable plant, and for this reason is more expensive to buy. *T. sessile* has leaves of deep green, marbled grey. The usually maroon flowers are stemless, narrow, erect and pointed with slightly twisted petals. The stems are slightly shorter, at 10–12in (20–30cm), and they are produced from late spring.

T. chloropetalum has mottled leaves and cream-white flowers, whilst *T. luteum* has greenish-yellow blooms. *T. erectum* is a curious member of the family; with the common name of birthroot, or squawroot, it produces bright maroon-purple spring flowers and large three-lobed mid-green leaves.

ABOVE *Scilla mischtschenkoana*

ABOVE *Trillium grandiflorum* 'Flore Pleno' AGM

95

PERENNIAL PLANTS

Perennial plants, those that come up year after year, provide the most amount of colour in a shaded garden. Bulbs and annuals tend to have shorter flowering seasons, and trees and shrubs are not generally as floriferous (with one or two notable exceptions), so it is to the perennial plants that we should look to for our longer-lasting colour spectacles.

In the list of plants over the next 22 pages I have included border perennials and alpine perennials together – they are not necessarily mutually exclusive, and it is at the gardener's discretion whether, for example, a saxifrage plant is set out in a border or on a rockery. The following list comprises most of the shade-loving perennials that you are likely to need.

NAME: *ACONITUM* (MONKSHOOD)

Origin: Throughout the northern hemisphere
Shade preference: Light
USDA Zone: Z3–6
Description: All parts of the *Aconitum* plant are poisonous, in particular the roots. The distinctive hooded flowers have given rise to the common name of monkshood, but wolf's bane and helmet flower are also names given to these plants. Whilst they are at their best in an open, sunny position, provided a plentiful supply of moisture is present, they will also grow well in a lightly shaded spot.
Popular species and varieties: *Aconitum japonicum* produces deep violet-blue flowers, which really stand out against the vivid greenery of the leaves. There are also several excellent hybrids: *A. x cammarum* 'Bicolor' AGM, as its name suggests, has a distinctive combination of blue and white on branching stems. 'Spark's Variety' AGM was first introduced in the 19th century and has stood the test of time with its dark violet-blue flowers. 'Ivorine' is a vigorous, bushy plant with ivory white flowers on branching stems.

LEFT *Aconitum japonicum*

NAME: *AJUGA* (BUGLE)

Origin: Europe, Middle East
Shade preference: Dappled
USDA Zone: Z6
Description: Excellent ground-cover plant with attractive foliage and short spikes of blue or pink flowers in early summer. They like a moist soil, and will tolerate dappled shade; the deeper the shade the more likely it is that coloured-leaved forms will revert to all-green, and that fewer flowers will be produced.

Popular species and varieties: By far the most numerous members of this family in cultivation are varieties of *Ajuga reptans*, which produce flowers of royal blue over deep green leaves. The varieties have been bred for their rich leaf colourings, including 'Brauherz' AGM (purple bronze) and 'Burgundy Glow' AGM (maroon and cream, and light blue flowers); both grow to just 6in (15cm) or so in height. 'Catlin's Giant' AGM reaches 10in (25cm). 'Pink Elf' has glorious rich pink flowers.

NAME: *ALCHEMILLA MOLLIS* AGM (LADY'S MANTLE)

Origin: Worldwide, but most garden forms are of European origin
Shade preference: Dappled to dense
USDA Zone: Z5–7
Description: *Alchemilla mollis* AGM is the one form that is most likely to appear in our gardens, but there are many forms that occur in nature, far and wide. This garden plant has handsome green foliage and masses of yellow-green, feathery sprays of flowers that are carried over several weeks from early summer onwards. It is ideal for cutting and widely used by flower arrangers. The plant self-seeds, and once you have it you will find it cropping up in many and various places in the garden.

Popular species and varieties: 'Auslese' positively demands light shade, otherwise it performs poorly. It is grey-green and is a very sturdy plant. 'Robusta' is slightly taller, possibly up to 30in (75cm), and the denser the shade the more it seems to like it.

ABOVE *Ajuga* 'Pink Elf'

ABOVE *Alchemilla mollis* AGM

ABOVE *Anemone* 'Hadspen Abundance' AGM

ABOVE *Aruncus dioicus*

NAME: *ANEMONE x HYBRIDA* (JAPANESE ANEMONE)

Origin: Worldwide
Shade preference: Light
USDA Zone: Z6
Description: Japanese anemones are useful, long-lived plants, adding colour to the garden from late summer to late autumn. Once planted these hardy perennials can be left undisturbed for years, eventually building up into sizeable clumps. Although the same genus as the forms of *Anemone* discussed on page 82, these do not grow from tubers.
Popular species and varieties: 'Whirlwind' is a semi-double white form, whilst 'Königin Charlotte' AGM is semi-double and pink. *A. hupehensis* 'Hadspen Abundance' AGM is purple-pink, with flowers some 2in (5cm) across.

NAME: *ARUNCUS DIOICUS* (GOAT'S BEARD)

Origin: Western and Central Europe, Southern Russia
Shade preference: Light
USDA Zone: Z4
Description: This is a graceful, moisture-loving perennial that reaches a top height of some 6ft (2m), so is generally suited to larger gardens. The huge, cream-white flower plumes are spectacular, either in a border or at the side of a garden pond. *Aruncus dioicus* is a sizeable plant with broad, fern-like foliage, surmounted in the summer with strong 4ft (1.2m) stems carrying its eye-catching plumes.
Popular species and varieties: 'Kneifii' AGM is more in keeping with smaller gardens, reaching just 24in (60cm) in height. Although much smaller, it is every bit as desirable, with its finely divided leaves. 'Glasnevin' is sized between the two, at some 5ft (1.5m) high.

NAME: *ASTILBE*

Origin: Eastern Asia, North America
Shade preference: Light
USDA Zone: Z5–6
Description: Astilbes are popular perennials, and are frequently grown in unsuitably hot, dry, sunny places. Here they are lacklustre and produce spindly flowers. Without enough moisture and shade they can fall well short of their display potential. Flowering generally begins in early summer and the attractive plume-like heads of tiny flowers, which last for several weeks, ensure that the *Astilbe* owner has a good return on investment. The rusty brown seedheads produced in late summer and autumn are almost as effective as the flower spikes.

Popular species and varieties: There is plenty of choice. The hybrids borne out of *Astilbe x arendsii* are the most commonly seen, generally producing plumes up to 3ft (1m) in height. 'Fire' is often found under its German name 'Feuer', and produces a brilliant red flower. 'Bressingham Beauty' is bright pink, 'Anita Pfeifer' is sugar-pink, 'Harmony' is candyfloss-pink and 'Amethyst' is lilac-purple.

The species *A. simplicifolia* has added its quota too. 'Atrorosea' carries sheaves of tiny bright pink flowers over a long period of time. 'Bronce Elegans' AGM is a charming dark-leafed pink variety that is only 9in (23cm) high. 'Sprite' has dark leaves and masses of tiny, shell-pink flowers.

ABOVE *Astilbe* '**Harmony**'

NAME: *ASTRANTIA*

Origin: Central and Eastern Europe
Shade preference: Dappled to light
USDA Zone: Z6
Description: This popular perennial produces curiously shaped flowers comprising a dome of tiny florets surrounded by narrow, parchment-like bracts. This gives them a star-like appearance.
Popular species and varieties: The most widely seen species is *Astrantia major*, with starry, greenish white flowers on stems 24in (60cm) high. There are a number of very good varieties, including 'Claret' (deep, rich pink), 'Ruby Wedding' (deep red) and 'Shaggy' (extra large bracts of white, tipped green). 'Sunningdale Variegated' has leaves with white streaks; it is very effective early in the season, as the streaks fade when the flowers start to appear. *Astrantia maxima* AGM is, to some, the best species as its flowers are a lovely rose-pink with striking emerald green on the underside. However, this is also a vigorous plant and needs controlling.

NAME: *BERGENIA* (ELEPHANT'S EARS)

Origin: Eastern Asia
Shade preference: Light
USDA Zone: Z3
Description: With their leathery leaves, bergenias are some of the first hardy perennials to flower each year. Often the buds can be seen in late winter, just waiting for the right time to open. Some forms take on attractive autumn leaf colourings, and often these will continue throughout the winter, to be replaced by fresh green leaves in the spring. It is these large, rounded, tough leaves that have resulted in the plant's common name of elephant's ears. Bergenias are good ground-cover plants, and can be left undisturbed until they eventually become overcrowded. The flower stems are strong and each is topped with a flower head of pink, magenta, crimson or white.
Popular species and varieties: Many forms have been raised by plant breeders in Germany – *Bergenia x schmidtii* AGM has shiny foliage and pink flowers on stems 12in (30cm) high; 'Abendglut' (syn. 'Evening Glow') has magenta and crimson flowers over maroon winter foliage; 'Morgenrote' (syn. 'Morning Blush') AGM is deep carmine-pink; and 'Silberlicht' (syn. 'Silver Light') AGM has white flowers that take on a pinkish tinge as they age. The Irish-raised 'Ballawley' AGM is bright crimson. 'Bressingham White' and 'Bressingham Ruby' have flowers of white and ruby-red respectively, but the leaves of the former are bright green and of the latter are a lovely beetroot red.

LEFT *Astrantia major* 'Sunningdale Variegated'

ABOVE *Bergenia* 'Abendglut'

NAME: *BRUNNERA MACROPHYLLA* AGM (SIBERIAN BUGLOSS)

Origin: Eastern Europe to western Siberia

Shade preference: Dappled to light

USDA Zone: Z3

Description: These really hardy perennials, with their forget-me-not-like flowers, are excellent for ground cover. Easily grown in moist soil and in a shaded spot, even under trees, makes them particularly useful.

Popular species and varieties: *Brunnera macrophylla* AGM forms a dense mat of heart-shaped leaves, with sprays of blue flowers appearing in late spring. There are several named forms, including 'Langtrees' (syn. 'Aluminium Spot') with spots of silvery grey on the leaves. 'Jack Frost' is spectacularly variegated with leaves of silver and green veining; 'Dawson's White' (syn. 'Variegata') has white variegated leaves.

ABOVE *Brunnera macrophylla* AGM

101

ABOVE *Corydalis solida* subsp. *solida* 'George Baker' AGM

NAME: *CORYDALIS*

Origin: Europe, Asia, Tropical Africa
Shade preference: Dappled to light
USDA Zone: Z5–7
Description: Delicate, even flimsy-looking spring-flowering perennials, with attractive, long-lasting tubular flowers. The first forms to be grown were yellow, but plant breeders soon discovered that there was a good market for these plants, and that it was relatively easy to breed new colours into them. They are suitable for woodland gardens, lightly shaded borders and rock or alpine gardens.
Popular species and varieties: *C. flexuosa* has dark, finely cut foliage and blue-spurred flowers. There are several varieties available, including: 'China Blue' (light blue flowers); 'Purple Leaf' (blue-mauve flowers with a purplish tinge to the leaves); and 'Golden Panda' (blue flowers with

yellow leaves at their brightest in spring). *C. lutea*, with yellow flowers, is one of those plants that once you have in the garden you are unlikely to lose, for it seeds itself prodigiously. *C. solida* is a clump-forming plant growing from small underground tubers. In mid-spring spikes of pink, mauve, white or reddish purple flowers appear. An excellent form of this is *C. solida* subsp. *solida* 'George Baker' AGM, with flowers of an unusual brick-red colour.

NAME: *EPIMEDIUM* (BARRENWORT)

Origin: North Africa and Mediterranean
Shade preference: Light to dense
USDA Zone: Z5–7
Description: Mostly grown as ground cover plants, some have attractive foliage in spring, others in the summer, and others still in the autumn. They are moisture-lovers and will grow happily in shady spots – as long as they do not dry out. Grown primarily for their leaves, the tiny flowers are held on wiry stems, and are daintily attractive in their own right.
Popular species and varieties: *E. x perralchicum* 'Frohnleiten' AGM produces coppery red tinged leaves when young, and deep yellow flowers. *E. x rubrum* AGM has young spring foliage that is tinged with red, and then the crimson flowers appear; in autumn the foliage turns to orange and yellow. *E. alpinum* has reddish flowers and good autumn colour, whilst *E. pinnatum* subsp. *colchicum* AGM has yellow flowers and red-tinged foliage in autumn and winter. *E. x versicolor* 'Sulphureum' AGM is evergreen, with pale yellow flowers.

NAME: *GENTIANA* (GENTIAN)

Origin: North America, Europe, Eastern Asia, Himalayas, New Zealand
Shade preference: Light
USDA Zone: Z3–6
Description: The gentian is one of the most admired plants for a rock garden. The characteristic blue of the trumpet-shaped gentian

ABOVE *Epimedium x perralchicum* 'Frohnleiten' AGM

flower is legendary, but it is also possible to grow white, yellow, purple and red forms as well (although these are primarily sun-lovers). Gentians have a reputation of being difficult to grow and even more difficult to flower but this is not true of all species. Happily, the forms that are recommended for shadier places are among the easiest to grow.

Popular species and varieties: *G. sino-ornata* produces single blue flowers on creeping stems in autumn, whilst *G. makinoi* produces them at the tips of 24in (60cm) long stems in summer. The willow gentian (*G. asclepiadea*) has blue flowers in its leaf axils on arching stems, whilst *G. septemfida* keeps low, with tufts of blue trumpet-flowers throughout summer and autumn.

ABOVE *Gentiana septemfida*

ABOVE *Geranium psilostemon* AGM

NAME: *GERANIUM* (CRANESBILL)

Origin: North-eastern Turkey
Shade preference: Dappled to light
USDA Zone: Z6
Description: The *Geranium* genus is generally thought of as being the perfect plant for a sunny spot and, I suppose, this is largely true. The misapplied common name for the bedding geranium (more properly *Pelargonium*) certainly needs a position in full sun, and this is perhaps where the sun-loving reputation for any plants with the name *Geranium* has arisen. However, there are some very good perennial cranesbills that actually prefer growing in light shade.
Popular species and varieties: *G. psilostemon* AGM has bright magenta flowers and can easily reach 4ft (1.2m) in height, so unusually for a *Geranium* is better mid-way or at the back of a border. *G. sanguineum* (known as the bloody cranesbill) forms a low mat of small, divided, rounded leaves, topped by large numbers of purple-magenta flowers over a long period. *G. sanguineum var. striatum* AGM has graceful, light pink petals delicately veined with a deeper pink. *G. x magnificum* AGM has rich violet, darkly-veined saucer-shaped flowers.

NAME: *HABERLEA RHODOPENSIS* AGM

Origin: Eastern Europe
Shade preference: Dappled to light
USDA Zone: Z7
Description: *Haberlea* is a small genus of small evergreen perennial plants, grown for their elegant sprays of flowers. It is a useful rock garden or wall plant, but also likes a moist soil. It will flower in full sun, but produces a greater quantity of flowers if in dappled or light shade. *H. rhodopensis* AGM grows to just 4in (10cm) in height, and has a spread of just 6in (15cm) or so. The leaves have a fine layer of soft hairs on both sides. Sprays of funnel-shaped, blue-violet flowers, each with a white throat, appear on long stems in late spring and early summer.
Popular species and varieties: *H. rhodopensis* 'Virginalis' has beautiful flowers of pure white; *H. ferdinandi-coburgii* is very similar to *H. rhodopensis*, but the leaves are of a darker green, and hairy on the underside only.

ABOVE *Haberlea rhodopensis* **AGM**

NAME: *HELLEBORUS* (HELLEBORE)

Origin: Western and Central Europe, Russia
Shade preference: Dappled to light
USDA Zone: Z3–6
Description: Hellebores are addictive, such is their magic, especially the hybrids of *Helleborus orientalis*. Winter still has to release its grip when the first buds on hellebores start to expand. Christmas and Lenten roses are two widely-known common names, but these are by no means the only members of the family. Most hellebores will grow in full sun or light shade, but at all costs you should avoid growing them in places that are exposed to cold winds.

Popular species and varieties: The most popular hellebores are those known as the Oriental Hybrids, with a great many named varieties in a wide range of colours from almost black to purple, yellow, pink and white, some with plain flowers, others spotted and veined. Garden centres stock a good range, and it is best to see the plants in flower before making your choice. The stinking hellebore (*H. foetidus*), so-called because of the unpleasant smell coming from the foliage when crushed, is particularly useful for lightly shaded areas. It has pale green flowers and is a real beauty. Among the named forms is Wester Flisk Group, with reddish stems. The Christmas rose (*H. niger* AGM) has flat pure white flowers, occasionally with pinkish tones.

ABOVE *Helleborus foetidus*

105

ABOVE *Heuchera* 'Frosted Violet'

NAME: *HEUCHERA* (CORAL BELLS)

Origin: North America
Shade preference: Light
USDA Zone: Z4–9
Description: A considerable amount of breeding work has taken place with *Heuchera* over the past ten years or so. Grown primarily for their attractive leaves, the wispy flowers on wiry stems are of secondary importance.
Popular species and varieties: Most of the garden-worthy varieties today are hybrids. Look for 'Amber Waves' (yellow and bronze leaves), 'Chocolate Ruffles' (redish-purple and chocolate brown leaves) and 'Frosted Violet' (pinkish-violet leaves mottled silver in the spring, becoming bronze-purple in summer). 'Palace Purple Select' has bronze leaves and white flowers on stems 24in (60cm) high.

NAME: *HOSTA* (PLANTAIN LILY)

Origin: Japan, China, Korea
Shade preference: Light
USDA Zone: Z3
Description: These elegant plants are among the most popular of all hardy perennials. They are grown principally for their handsome

ABOVE *Hosta sieboldiana*

foliage, which is produced in a range of shapes, sizes and colours. In summer the plants produce strong stems with mostly trumpet-shaped flowers, varying from pale lilac or mauve to white. Leaf size is very variable, from those with huge affairs 12in (30cm) or more across and long, to the small-leaved types of just 2in (5cm). The variegated forms are the most popular with cream, white, gold and blue markings on the leaves. Hostas tend to perform very well in both full sun and in light shade. If you grow them in the latter, however, individual leaves may be larger, and the flower stems will be taller, although the number of blooms will be reduced.

Popular species and varieties: More than a thousand cultivars and varieties mean that the choice is formidable. Two hybrids with very large leaves and pale mauve flowers are 'Big Daddy' (puckered, heart-shaped, shiny blue leaves) and 'Zounds' (with an almost metallic sheen to the green-yellow leaves). 'Bright Lights' has leaves of mid-green with a darker blue-green edge. 'Sagae' has leaves that are green-centred, with gold edges; lavender-blue flowers appear in mid-summer. 'Golden Tiara' AGM is a classic, fast-growing hosta with green-centred leaves, edged with gold. *H. sieboldiana* is a variable plant making a large 24in (60cm) tall mound, with large, oval leaves with rippled edges; colours vary from mid-green to deep blue-green. *H. ventricosa* AGM produces bold, shiny, dark green leaves and purple summer flowers. *H. ventricosa* var. *aureomaculata*, meanwhile, has spring leaves that are splashed with gold in the centre, but be warned that they revert to all-green by summer.

ABOVE *Lamium* 'Pink Pewter'

NAME: *LAMIUM MACULATAUM* (SPOTTED DEAD NETTLE)

Origin: Mediterranean
Shade preference: Light to dense
USDA Zone: Z3–6
Description: The most widely grown forms are varieties of *Lamium maculatum*, the spotted dead nettle, which is a useful hardy perennial for ground cover, successful particularly in shaded spots under large trees. The straight species has green foliage, each leaf having a silver stripe down the middle. It also carries deep, purplish pink flowers from late spring to late summer.
Popular species and varieties: Among the numerous varieties available is 'Aureum' (golden leaves and pink flowers); 'Beacon Silver' (silvery foliage and bright, deep pink flowers); 'Pink Pewter' (leaves of silver-green, edged green, and flowers of salmon-pink); and 'White Nancy' AGM (white flowers and silver leaves).

NAME: *LYSIMACHIA (LOOSESTRIFE)*

Origin: Central Europe, Asia
Shade preference: Light
USDA Zone: Z5
Description: The *Lysimachia* is a hardy perennial for which a spot should be chosen with care. It can be invasive, especially if growing on a moist soil, which it loves. In the right position this is an excellent, very colourful plant, at home in full sun or light shade.
Popular species and varieties: *L. punctata* is a vigorous plant, producing spikes of brassy yellow flowers on 36in (90cm) tall stems in summer. Even taller, at 4ft (1.2m), is *L. clethroides* AGM, a native of China and Japan; it produces whitish flowers from late summer onwards. *L. nummularia* (known as creeping Jenny), creeps along the ground and can be spectacular along the base of a hedge (which tells you that this species does not mind dry soil). The golden-leaved form 'Aurea' is attractive in its own right, but is less floriferous. Be warned that both of these forms can be invasive, and need regular controlling.

ABOVE *Lysimachia punctata*

NAME: *LYTHRUM* (PURPLE LOOSESTRIFE)

Origin: North-eastern US

Shade preference: Light

USDA Zone: Z3

Description: *Lythrum* is a moisture-loving plant that grows happily in good, moisture-retentive soil, either in full sun or light shade. Easily grown and very adaptable, it will even tolerate – and is recommended for – boggy conditions.

Popular species and varieties: The reddish purple flower spikes of *Lythrum salicaria* brighten up the banks of streams and ponds. There are several excellent named forms, one being 'Feuekerze' AGM, with 4ft (1.2m) spikes of rosy red flowers. 'Robert' is a sturdy variety with blooms of clear pink; 'Blush' is light pink; and 'Zigeunerblut' is deep carmine red.

ABOVE *Lythrum salicaria*

ABOVE *Meconopsis cambrica*

NAME: *MECONOPSIS*

Origin: The Himalayas, China, Western Europe
Shade preference: Dappled to light
USDA Zone: Z6
Description: The blue Himalayan poppy (*Meconopsis betonicifolia* AGM) enjoys considerable popularity, but is just one of some exquisite, though occasionally challenging species. There are white, pink, red and yellow forms as well, and they all enjoy the dappled or partial shade of a woodland garden.
Popular species and varieties: *M. betonicifolia* AGM produces sky-blue to rose-lavender blooms in mid-summer, frequently up to ten flowers per stalk. The form *M. betonicifolia* var. *alba* is pure white. The Welsh poppy (*M. cambrica*) produces its deeply cupped yellow flowers from mid-spring to early autumn. *M. cambrica* var. *aurantiaca* is orange; 'Flora Pleno' is yellow-orange and semi-double; and 'Frances Perry' is deep orange-crimson. Reddy pink is the colour given to the blooms of *M. napaulensis*, which appear in mid-summer.

NAME: *PODOPHYLLUM* (CUSTARD APPLE)

Origin: China
Shade preference: Dappled to light
USDA Zone: Z7
Description: The *Podophyllum*, whilst not a common plant, provides some of the most colourful and highly textural leaves on any woodland perennial.
Popular species and varieties: *P. delavayi* is a fabulous woodland plant with large, broad rounded leaves in tones of burgundy, green and black and with a satin-like surface. Reddish pink flowers, generally held under the leaves, are of minor importance. Actually, they smell rather of rotting meat – attracting flies as pollinating insects – but do not be put off by this. *P. pleianthum* features pairs of large, glossy green leaves that can be 18in (45cm) across. In early summer clusters of small blood-red, balloon-shaped flowers appear immediately at or slightly above the juncture of the two leaves.

ABOVE *Podophyllum pleianthum*

NAME: *POLYGONATUM x HYBRIDUM* (SOLOMON'S SEAL)

Origin: Throughout the northern hemisphere
Shade preference: Dappled to dense
USDA Zone: Z6
Description: The *Polygonatum* genus contains a varied range of attractive and elegant woodland plants, usually grown in gardens as specimen clumps or ground cover. They vary from tall, swarthy clumps of gracefully nodding stems to small, yet vigorous, ground-covering colonies. The usually small, pendulous, bell-shaped flowers, often white but sometimes pink, are produced in clusters at regular positions along the flower stem. These are classic plants for the shady garden.

Popular species and varieties: The straight *P. x hybridum* is by far the most commonly grown species; its white flowers really stand out against a dark and shaded backdrop, such as that provided by a conifer hedge. 'Betburg' produces rich purple-brown flowers; and 'Striatum' has creamy-white streaks to the leaves.

ABOVE *Polygonatum x hybridum*

ABOVE *Primula* Gold Laced Group

NAME: *PRIMULA (PRIMROSE)*

Origin: Throughout the northern hemisphere, southern South America
Shade preference: Dappled to dense
USDA Zone: Z5–6
Description: Whichever plants you grow in your shady garden there should be room for a *Primula* – or ten! This genus ranks as one of the largest, most variable, durable and likeable of all plant genera. There are primulas for growing in pots, on rockeries, in flowerbeds, in woodland dells and at the sides of a pond. Slightly shaded places are best, and they prefer a fairly rich, organic, slightly acid soil.
Popular species and varieties: The common or wild primrose (*P. vulgaris*), makes a fine addition to a shaded border, but is perhaps most at home within a wild area in longish, uncut grass. The blooms of *P. vulgaris* subsp. *sibthorpii* are pink, or occasionally white. *P. japonica* is possibly the best known of the 'candelabra' primulas (meaning that it bears its flowers in rounded clusters, or whorls, at intervals along the main central stem). It has lush leaves and several tiers of red, pink or white flowers opening at stages throughout early and mid-summer. Four of the best varieties are: 'Alba' (white); 'Apple Blossom' (pink); 'Miller's Crimson' (deep pink); and 'Postford White' (white). Other candelabra primulas include *P. aurantiaca* (orange, or orange-red), *P. beesiana* (deep red with yellow centres), *P. x bulleesiana* (in a wide range of colours from yellow, orange and pink through to red and purple) and *P. pulverulenta* (pale pink or mauve). The relatively small flowers of the Gold Laced Group are dark red to deep chocolate brown, with each petal edged in golden-yellow. It is a stunning plant for a cool, damp spot in partial shade.

NAME: *PULMONARIA (LUNGWORT)*

Origin: Europe
Shade preference: Dappled to light
USDA Zone: Z3–6
Description: The *Pulmonaria* genus goes by a number of common names, including lungworts, Josephs and Maries, the Good Friday plant, thunder and lightning, soldiers and sailors and Jerusalem sage. The small, five-petalled flowers are familiar in spring gardens, and later the typically spotted leaves make a pleasing addition to shady borders. There are ten species, all of which are small herbaceous plants with short flower stems. Leaves are usually oval or oblong, never divided, and are roughly hairy, like all other parts of the plant. The foliage may be green or sometimes marked with silvery spots and blotches.
Popular species and varieties: *P. angustifolia* AGM has plain, pale green leaves, which emerge early and contrast well with the mid-blue flowers. *P. angustifolia* 'Munstead Blue' has light green unspotted leaves and bright blue flowers. *P. saccharata* is an attractive plant from France

ABOVE *Pulmonaria* 'Mawson's Blue'

and Italy and has large leaves that are heavily spotted, and leafy flower stems with purplish blooms. The best cultivars are considered to be those with the most silvered leaves, which include the 'Argentea Group' AGM.

The hybrid 'Roy Davidson' has narrow leaves, lightly spotted in silver; its flowers are mid-blue fading to pink. 'Mawson's Blue' has plain unspotted green leaves with rich, dark blue flowers appearing in mid-spring.

NAME: *RODGERSIA AESCULIFOLIA*

Origin: China
Shade preference: Light
USDA Zone: Z5
Description: This is one of those plants that looks perfect next to a woodland stream or large pond, but incongruous when grown anywhere else in the garden. Its leaves look as if they should be growing high up on a horse chestnut tree, but this plant is, of course, a border perennial. Lovers of bold, dramatic, architectural plants will adore it. In mid-summer, plumes of many tiny pinkish-red blossoms are held well above the foliage.

ABOVE *Rodgersia aesculifolia*

Popular species and varieties: *R. pinnata* 'Superba' has deeply divided leaves and white flowers. *R. sambucifolia* has leaves like an elder and white flowers. *R. podophylla* produces palm-shaped leaves and cream flowers.

NAME: *ROSCOEA*

Origin: China
Shade preference: Dappled to light
USDA Zone: Z6–7
Description: This is a small genus of charming little plants, related to the ginger. Their exotic foliage and flowers brings a touch of the tropics to our gardens. You may find them difficult to get hold of, however. They are not for deep shade, but they do well in woodland conditions where they are of considerable value, flowering later than many of the other plants that grow there. They can also be grown well on rock gardens.
Popular species and varieties: *R. cautleoides* AGM has narrow upright leaves and small clusters of usually pale yellow hooded flowers produced in late summer. The cultivar 'Kew Beauty' AGM has flowers of darker yellow. *R. purpurea* has similar rich green foliage and attractive blooms of usually purple, mauve or even white. *R. humeana* AGM is the most robust species with rich green oval leaves and purple flowers from late spring into summer.

NAME: *SAXIFRAGA* (SAXIFRAGE)

Origin: Worldwide, in mountainous zones
Shade preference: Dappled to light
USDA Zone: Z3–7
Description: Most of the small alpine saxifrages are sun-lovers, but there are larger species that are becoming more widely grown and are perfect for the front of shady beds and borders.

ABOVE *Roscoea humeana* AGM

Popular species and varieties: *S. fortunei* is a leafy plant rather similar in appearance to a *Heuchera*, but the foliage is glossier and somewhat succulent in appearance. Dainty white, star-shaped blooms are carried in airy masses on long stems in late autumn. The variety 'Black Ruby' has almost black leaves and pink flowers. The plant commonly known as mother-of-thousands (*S. stolonifera*) is often grown as a house plant, but it will in fact grow outside in sheltered positions, where it will form an attractive ground-cover plant; its evergreen oval leaves spreading freely. The hybrid plant *S.* 'Stansfieldii' produces lovely rose-pink flowers with yellow-green centres.

ABOVE *Saxifraga* **'Stansfieldii'**

NAME: *SYMPHYTUM* (COMFREY)

Origin: Europe to Middle East
Shade preference: Light
USDA Zone: Z5
Description: If you have an awkward, dry, shady part of the garden, it is almost guaranteed that *Symphytum* will survive there. This low, ground-covering perennial is able to grow in relatively poor conditions, even next to evergreen hedges. They come into their own in spring when they produce showy clusters of drooping flowers in a range of colours, although most are white. The oval leaves are bristly. The plant is good at suppressing weeds when used as ground cover.
Popular species and varieties: There are some particularly attractive variegated selections but these need a little more light to make them grow well. *S. ibericum* has broadly oval, sharply pointed leaves; the flowers have a reddish hue in bud, opening to pale yellow. 'All Gold' has leaves of a rich golden-yellow in spring, turning green in summer; flowers pink-mauve.

ABOVE *Symphytum*

115

ABOVE *Tiarella cordifolia* AGM

NAME: *TIARELLA* (FOAMFLOWER)

Origin: North America
Shade preference: Dappled to dense
USDA Zone: Z3
Description: Tiarellas are cultivated chiefly for their clumps of handsome foliage, somewhat like small *Heuchera*. However, from late spring onwards short spikes of little frothy pink-white flowers appear. It will tolerate quite deep shade but will only form a good thick, bushy growth if the soil is moist and fertile.

Popular species and varieties: *T. cordifolia* AGM carries evergreen heart-shaped leaves, each with 3–5 shallow lobes and faintly streaked, striped or mottled scarlet to maroon, or sometimes plain green. White to pale pink flowers are carried in striking upright spikes in spring. *T. wherryi* is the species most often seen in cultivation. It has starry flowers of pale pink.

NAME: *UVULARIA GRANDIFLORA* AGM (MERRYBELLS)

Origin: North America
Shade preference: Dappled to light
USDA Zone: Z5
Description: The dainty, pale yellow, dangling, bell-shaped flowers of this woodland perennial have long, twisted petals and hang from slender, rather arching stems that reach only 12in (30cm), or less, in height. They appear in mid- to late spring. The leaves are narrow, oval and greyish green. It will not thrive if grown in a container as it needs a free root run and cooler soil than can be achieved in pot-growing.

Popular species and varieties: *Uvularia grandiflora* AGM is the most commonly seen form, but *U. grandiflora* var. *pallida* with its even paler yellow blooms is worth a try. *U. sessilifolia* is the smallest species with pale yellow to straw-coloured flowers in spring and early summer.

ABOVE *Uvularia grandiflora* AGM

NAME: *VIOLA* (VIOLET)

Origin: Warm, temperate climates worldwide, although there are some forms found in the tropics, yet others in the Arctic region.

Shade preference: Most enjoy full sun, but the two forms described here prefer dappled shade

USDA Zone: Z3–4

Description: The leaves of all forms of *Viola* are loosely heart-shaped, in many cases enlarging once the showy spring flowering has finished. Plant them in borders under larger shrubs, or bush roses as an attractive carpet.

Popular species and varieties: *V. cornuta* AGM (the horned violet) makes good ground cover in light shade. *V. cornuta* 'Alba Minor' has white flowers. *V. cucullata* AGM is known as the marsh blue violet, the flowers being held well above the leaves. The Labrador violet (*V. labradorica*) is a deciduous clump-former, with violet-blue spring flowers.

ABOVE *Viola labradorica*

GRASSES AND GRASS-LIKE PLANTS

Any plant with grass-like leaves tends to be called a grass. But just because it looks like a grass does not mean to say that it is botanically. Technically, grasses should be related to each other, all belonging to the huge *Gramineae* plant family (which contains more than 600 genera and some 9,000 species). *Gramineae* is divided into many sub-family groups, three of which are listed below.

There are four types of grass and grass-like plants that are commonly grown in gardens:

1 Common grasses and bamboos (members of the *Poaceae* sub-family); stems are round and hollow. Bamboos are simply woody-stemmed and often very tall grasses.

2 Sedges (*Cyperaceae*); stems are solid and triangular in cross-section.

3 Rushes (*Juncaceae*); stems are flat or cylindrical; all leaves arise from the base of the plant.

4 Acorus (*Araceae*); not even closely related to grass; leaves are carried in flattened fans, and the flowers are very clearly different from any of the grasses.

Below are details of the commonly grown *Acorus*, but all others covered are related, shade-tolerant grasses.

ABOVE *Acorus calamus* 'Argenteostriatus'

NAME: *ACORUS* (SWEET FLAG, OR SWEET RUSH)

Origin: North America, Asia, Europe
Shade preference: Dappled to dense
USDA Zone: Z4–5

Description: Technically this is neither a grass, nor a bamboo, yet it has the appearance of both – which is why I have elected to include it in this section rather than the Perennials section. It is actually a member of the *Arum* family. Its flowers, although not showy, are typical of the arum's 'spathes'. All forms of *Acorus* are usually found close to water, and the narrow, flat, grass-like leaves come from the root area in a distinct fan-shape, unlike any grass.

Popular species and varieties: Two main species are generally available. The green leaves of *A. calamus* will reach 18in (45cm) in length. The form 'Argenteostriatus' (often sold as 'Variegatus') has leaves of half-green and half-cream. The cream part may be tinged pink if the plant is being stressed, such as the conditions being cool, or the soil too dry. *A. gramineus* is

ABOVE *Carex elata 'Aurea'* AGM

ABOVE *Chusquea culeou* 'Tenuis'

the second species, and the forms usually seen are 'Variegatus' (green leaves with a central white stripe), 'Oborozuki' (yellow-gold leaves with slight green striping) and 'Ogon' (half-green, half-white).

NAME: *CAREX* (SEDGE)

Origin: Worldwide, especially the temperate and Arctic regions
Shade preference: Dappled to dense
USDA Zone: Z5–7
Description: Either densely tufted plants, or looser with creeping rhizomes, members of the large *Carex* genus are grown primarily for their foliage, even though the flowers are significant. Male and female flowers are carried separately, but on the same stem; the female ones resembling little brown cones. Many of the kinds available have foliage that is essentially brown; this tended to be ignored by gardeners a hundred years ago, but with the subtler styles enjoyed by today's gardeners, these plants have become very popular.
Popular species and varieties: By far the most frequently grown form is *C. elata* 'Aurea' AGM, known as Bowles' golden sedge. Its golden leaf colouring means that it is not appropriate for the

darkest of places; it should really be sited in full sun or dappled shade. Shadier places can be used for growing *C. conica* 'Snowline', narrow white margins to deep green leaves; *C. saxatilis* 'Ski Run', contorted leaves striped with white – just 4in (10cm) high; and *C. grayi*, known as the mace sedge, with long-lasting fresh green leaves and pale green seed heads.

NAME: *CHUSQUEA* (CHILEAN BAMBOO)

Origin: Mexico, as far south as Chile
Shade preference: Dappled to dense
USDA Zone: Z7
Description: A tall bamboo – up to 12ft (3.6m) tall, and slightly larger in width when fully grown – with thick, solid culms of green yellow. The short leaves on densely clustered branches are attractive, especially at the point when they combine with the current year's shoots ready to burst from their protective white sheaths. Gardeners choosing to grow this should think of it in the same way as a shrub, either as a lawn specimen or towards the back of a border.
Popular species and varieties: The most commonly seen forms are varieties of *C. culeou* AGM, particularly 'Tenuis' (bright green) and 'Purple Splendour' (reddish tinges to the leaves).

NAME: *HAKONECHLOA* (HAKONE GRASS)

Origin: Japan
Shade preference: Dappled
USDA Zone: Z5
Description: In 1990 hardly anyone had ever heard of this grass, but in the years that have passed it has endeared itself to more gardeners across the world than any other grass. It is a fairly low-growing Japanese grass, with soft, broad leaves; in some forms the variegations and leaf stripes are some of the most striking to be found on any garden plant. In common with most variegated plants, these forms will not tolerate dense shade, but at the edge of a shaded border it can be absolutely stunning.

Popular species and varieties: There are two commonly available forms. The best is, arguably, *H. macra* 'Aureola' AGM. It is frequently confused with 'Alboaurea' AGM, by experts as much as amateurs. Both have vivid golden yellow leaves, most of which contain a few narrow stripes of darker green; in 'Alboaurea', however, there is sometimes the merest hint of white striping. 'All Gold', as the name suggests, has leaves of all over yellow.

ABOVE *Hakonechloa macra* 'Aureola' AGM

ABOVE *Luzula sylvatica 'Aurea'*

ABOVE *Milium effusum 'Aureum'* AGM

NAME: *LUZULA* (WOODRUSH)

Origin: Worldwide, but especially the temperate parts of Eastern Europe and Western Asia

Shade preference: Light to dense

USDA Zone: Z4–6

Description: A useful rush for wet or dry shade, forms of *Luzula* are marked out by the fine white hairs on the leaves and the delicate spring flowers. They make good, decorative ground cover for woodland and shady bog gardens.

Popular species and varieties: *L. sylvatica* is known as the great woodrush, and there are many good varieties of this: 'Aurea' (upright grower with acid greenish-yellow leaves in the winter and spring, becoming greener in summer); 'Auslese' (light green leaves that are twisted at the tips); 'Marginata' (green leaves narrowly edged in white); and 'Taggart's Cream' (the new leaves emerge white, with thin green edges, and then become green).

NAME: *MILIUM EFFUSUM* (WOOD MILLET)

Origin: Temperate regions of the northern hemisphere

Shade preference: Dappled

USDA Zone: Z5

Description: A graceful woodland grass with loose tufts of flat, sometimes pointed leaves, and airy sprays of late spring flowers. It used to be grown as food for game birds.

Popular species and varieties: *M. effusum* 'Aureum' AGM, known as Bowles' golden grass (and not to be confused with the similar sounding common name for *Carex elata* 'Aurea') is highly popular. Bright yellow leaves and flowers in early spring to early summer, fading to pale yellow green as the weather hots up. Unlike most cultivated varieties, it comes true from seed. Another form, 'Yaffle', has green leaves with a narrow, central yellow line.

ABOVE *Pleioblastus variegatus* 'Tsuboii'

NAME: *PLEIOBLASTUS*

Origin: China, Japan
Shade preference: Dappled to dense
USDA Zone: Z7
Description: One of the larger types of bamboo, most forms of *Pleioblastus* are rampantly invasive, being spread by running rhizomes along and under the ground. The smaller and daintier species can be controlled in most gardens, however, or successfully confined in pots, provided the plants are repotted and divided each year. Most *Pleioblastus* are forest dwellers in their natural habitats, so are shade-tolerant but, as ever, the variegated forms need relatively brighter conditions if they are to show the leaf colourings at their best.

Popular species and varieties: The most popular form is *P. variegatus* 'Tsuboii' (often sold as *P. shibuyanus* 'Tsuboii'); it reaches 6ft (2m) in height but is usually much smaller. Its broad leaves are of fresh apple green, marked with wide bands of cream. *P. viridistriatus* is a fine yellow-variegated bamboo, with rich golden leaves striped with green. A cultivar of it, 'Chrysophyllus', is much slower growing, and is prone to scorching if planted in a sunny place.

ABOVE *Sasa veitchii*

ABOVE *Schoenoplectus lacustris* subsp. *tabernaemontani* 'Albescens'

NAME: *SASA*

Origin: Japan, Korea, China
Shade preference: Dappled to dense
USDA Zone: Z8
Description: A broad-leaved bamboo with distinctive pale edges to the leaves. This is due to a withdrawal of colour from the current year's foliage later in the season, rather than being a true variegation, although this is the overall effect. It can be invasive, so is recommended for large gardens only.
Popular species and varieties: Although there are a number of less significant forms, the only one of real garden merit is *S. veitchii*, which grows to some 4ft (1.2m) in height and spread. It will make a useful, low-growing hedge.

NAME: *SCHOENOPLECTUS* (BULL RUSH OR CLUB RUSH)

Origin: Worldwide
Shade preference: Dappled to dense
USDA Zone: Z4
Description: A moisture-loving grass of the rush (*Cyperaceae*) family. Erect, often architecturally good stems grow from vigorous root systems. Will grow happily in water, at pond margins as well as in marshes or boggy, infertile soil. In smaller ponds and bog gardens restrict these plants by growing them in containers, using a heavy clay soil.
Popular species and varieties: The candy or white rush (*S. lacustris* subsp. *tabernaemontani* 'Albescens') produces slender stems that are vertically striped white and pale peppermint-green, especially on new growth. They become greener as summer progresses. 'Zebrinus' has stems with horizontal bands of dark green and cream.

FERNS

Hardy ferns are enjoying high popularity today; 30 years ago it was very different. Then they were seen as boring green plants that were simply able to grow in a shady corner where nothing else would survive. The last bit was frequently true – they could be planted in some of the most inhospitable places, including dry shade, and they would thrive. That they were 'boring' is unfair and modern garden designers regularly include them in planting schemes today for their architecturally interesting foliage.

Ferns belong to the 'early morning' of the Earth, they are some of the first greenery that the planet ever saw, and I'm pleased to say that they exist much now as they did a hundred million years ago. Ferns are not flowering plants, reproducing instead through the production of spores. They are good plants for a woodland garden, and will make a newly planted one instantly look as though it has been there since the creation of time. Some types will grow out of cracks in stone in a shady basement garden, whilst others thrive on the side of a vast pond or lake.

ABOVE *Adiantum pedatum* AGM

NAME: *ADIANTUM* (MAIDENHAIR FERN)

Origin: Worldwide
Shade preference: Light to dense
USDA Zone: Z3–9
Description: This is a delicate-looking yet remarkably tough fern, and an essential feature of the shady garden. The wiry leaf stalks are shiny and black, and support large, often fan-shaped fronds. New fronds appear early in spring, sometimes contributing subtle purplish or pink colouring. Although these may appear alarmingly early, it is rare to see significant frost damage. The spores are formed on the folded margin of the edge of each leaf segment.
Popular species and varieties: The Eastern maidenhair (*A. pedatum* AGM) is deciduous, broadly fan-shaped with pale green leaves; it has a spreading habit but, having said that, only tends to reach up to 14in (35cm) across. *A. aleuticum* 'Japonicum' is similar but is slightly smaller, has slightly bluer leaves – but in spring the foliage is a lovely shade of rust-red. The Himalayan maidenhair (*A. venustum* AGM) is yellow-green, and is rather more sun-tolerant than the others mentioned.

NAME: *ATHYRIUM FILIX-FEMINA* AGM (LADY FERN)

Origin: Worldwide, but especially Eastern Asia
Shade preference: Dappled to dense
USDA Zone: Z3–6
Description: Easy to grow and graceful in appearance, the athyriums grow in most woodlands. Most species are deciduous with thin-textured, arching fronds. The spores are produced in short, straight or J-shaped structures on the undersides of the fronds. The spring, when the leaves are unfurling, is a favourite but short-lived time.
Popular species and varieties: *A. niponicum* var. *pictum* AGM is known as the Japanese painted fern; the fronds are lance-shaped and arching. The straight species is a plain light green, but some of the plants have greyish fronds with a purple midrib, and have been given the name pictum.

ABOVE *Athyrium niponicum* var. *pictum* AGM

NAME: *MATTEUCCIA STRUTHIOPTERIS* AGM (OSTRICH PLUME)

Origin: Most of the temperate regions of the northern hemisphere
Shade preference: Dappled to light
USDA Zone: Z3–7
Description: Also known as the shuttlecock fern, this plant can be invasive. It has a reputation for being a bit of a thug, as it will grow and multiply if it is happy with its soil and growing environment. However, if you have the space it is a 'must'. It is deciduous, but come spring the new fronds unfurl in gold and bronze tints before becoming the freshest of lime greens. Its fronds can measure up to 5ft (1.5m) from tip to base.
Popular species and varieties: *M. orientalis* is similar to *M. struthiopteris*, but is smaller at just 32in (80cm) or so. *M. pensylvanica* AGM has fronds that are near black when unfurling; a very invasive species.

ABOVE *Matteuccia struthiopteris* AGM

ABOVE *Onoclea sensibilis* AGM

NAME: *ONOCLEA SENSIBILIS* AGM (SENSITIVE FERN)

Origin: Asia, America
Shade preference: Dappled to light
USDA Zone: Z2
Description: This is a lovely fern, reaching about 2ft (60cm) high. The triangular fronds have a pinkish tinge when they first open. Sadly, however, these fronds are most sensitive – hence its common name – to autumn frosts. Although the plant is as hardy as anything (it is listed as being Z2) the fronds are not.
Popular species and varieties: *Onoclea* is widely regarded as a single-species genus, but experts disagree over this. Therefore you may be able to find a species *O. intermedia*, which is the same as *O. sensibilis*, but slightly smaller. *O. sensibilis* Copper Form is hard to find but worth the search, as its new fronds in spring are, for a brief period, bright red.

NAME: *OSMUNDA REGALIS* (THE ROYAL FERN)

Origin: Most of the temperate regions of the northern hemisphere
Shade preference: Dappled to light
USDA Zone: Z2
Description: This is generally considered to be the best fern for pond side or bog garden planting and it is, arguably, the most impressive

of all the hardy deciduous ferns. It was once common in the wild wet fens and marsh banks of Europe, but is now most often seen in gardens. It is a highly desirable plant for large pond and streamside situations, although some of the cultivated forms are less demanding of space. The lime green, prettily divided fronds first appear as copper-tinted crooked shoots in spring, and finally turn yellow and bronze in autumn. Smaller, stiffer, spore-bearing fronds arise from the centre of the plant.

Popular species and varieties: Closely related forms include *O. regalis* 'Purpurascens', with purple-green stems and fronds, and markedly pink-brown young shoots; the crested royal fern ('Cristata') and 'Undulata' are both smaller, and have attractively tasselled foliage.

NAME: *POLYSTICHUM* (SHIELD FERN)

Origin: Most of the temperate regions of the world
Shade preference: Light
USDA Zone: Z3–8
Description: These plants usually give year-round interest to a garden. The spore-bearing organs on the underside of the frond are covered by a round, shield-shaped structure attached in the centre, hence the common name. In most garden-worthy types the young growth in spring is conspicuous by its attractive covering of gingery or silvery scales. Most *Polystichum* are evergreen.

Popular species and varieties: *P. aculeatum* forms a round clump of fronds, usually 2–3ft (60–90cm) across, and in maturity is a rich, dark green. The soft shield fern (*P. setiferum*) is bigger at some 5ft (1.5m) long; *P. setiferum* 'Acutilobum' has narrow, more pointed fronds; and *P. setiferum* Dahlem Group have fronds that are apple-green, upright and more densely leafy towards the base.

ABOVE *Osmunda regalis*

ABOVE *Polystichum setiferum* Dahlem Group

CLIMBING PLANTS

There will always be a side of your house that is shadier than the others. For every garden wall and fence there is a shady side and a sunny side. These are facts of life. So how can a gardener make the most of these shady spots? Today, garden sizes are getting smaller and smaller and we frequently have to pick and choose our plants with care, to avoid the problem of them outgrowing the spaces we have given them. One way to increase the plant quotient in a small garden is to grow 'upwards'. More and more gardeners are clothing their walls, as well as the ground, with colour and foliage.

There are, by definition, few climbing plants that thrive in shade. This is because, over the millennia these plants have evolved to grow upwards, searching out the light, because this is what they need. Fortunately there are a few types that are lagging behind the rest evolutionarily speaking, and so are more appropriate for shady situations. But, having said that, there are none that are ideal in dense shade; if planted here they will simply grow longer stems in search of the sun, and both the form, and any ornamental display it has, will be spoilt. The following, however, are worth trying in dappled or light shade.

ABOVE *Clematis montana var. rubens* climbing through a conifer tree.

NAME: *CLEMATIS ALPINA*

Origin: Northern Europe, Russia
Shade preference: Dappled to light
USDA Zone: Z5
Description: There can be no coverage of climbing plants without the inclusion of *Clematis*. Known as the 'queen of climbers', the genus includes some quite beautiful flowering plants, and for almost every garden situation. Unfortunately, shade tolerance is perhaps the attribute least commonly given to them. Although the normal rule for *Clematis* is that the 'top of the plant should be in the sun, and the roots should be in the shade', it is fair to say that many of the popular summer-flowering hybrids offer their best flower-colour when the head of the plant is lightly shaded; intense sunlight can quickly fade and scorch the blooms.
Popular species and varieties: In terms of a dappled or light shade situation, there are really just four species that are successful, with the best being the early-flowering *Clematis alpina* and its forms. The late-flowering *C. tangutica* and *C. viticella* are also good in dappled shade. Of *C. alpina* the following are recommended:

'Frances Rivis' AGM (large flowers of pale blue), 'Rosy Pagoda' (pale pink), 'White Moth' (double flowers of white) and 'Pamela Jackman' AGM (strong mid-blue). Of *C. viticella* the following two are excellent: 'Mme Julia Correvon' AGM (dark red) and 'Royal Velours' AGM (deep purple). *C. tangutica* 'Gravetye Variety' and 'Bill Mackenzie' AGM (both yellow) are very fine plants. Also, although the popular rambling *Clematis montana var. rubens,* which can be planted to grow through trees, is not usually seen recommended for shade situations, I know for a fact that it is a fine plant for shade as I grew it on a north-facing house wall, which provided a spectacular of colour every spring, and I currently have one that is almost 40ft (12m) high, growing through a 60ft (18m) high Christmas tree. The first one received just a little late afternoon sun during the summer, whilst the second is growing in a situation of constant dappled light.

NAME: *HEDERA* (IVY)

Origin: Europe, Asia, North Africa
Shade preference: Dappled to dense
USDA Zone: Z5–8
Description: The ivy, in many western countries, must rank as one of the most commonly found climbers. No plant, climber or not, is associated more with shade than the ivy. There are few other types of plant that rival it as an evergreen cover for the ground or vertical structures, both natural (such as trees and tree stumps) and decorative (walls, fences, arches and pergolas). The often-made comment that these plants are dull actually annoys me. When I was a child my father, a professional horticulturist, had to create a collection of ivies for the world-famous Chelsea Flower Show. He gathered more than 400 species and varieties and some of them were the prettiest and daintiest of variegated foliage plants I have ever seen. Ivies have aerial roots, enabling them to climb and adhere to the structure, without the need for tying in.

ABOVE *Hedera colchica* 'Dentata Variegata' AGM

Popular species and varieties: There are two main groups of ivies: the large-leaved, more tender *Hedera colchica* and *H. canariensis*, and the small-leaved types, of which *Hedera helix* is the most important. Among the first species none are better than 'Sulphur Heart' AGM (pale green leaves with paler green and yellow blotches) and 'Dentata Variegata' AGM (leaves of mid-green and cream). *H. canariensis* 'Gloire de Marengo' AGM (dark green leaves with silver-grey surround and white margins) is also wonderful. Among the smaller leaf types, one of the best is 'Oro di Bogliasco' (green leaves with a golden central blotch); also excellent are 'Buttercup' and 'Glacier' AGM.

NAME: *HYDRANGEA PETIOLARIS* (CLIMBING HYDRANGEA)

Origin: USSR, Japan, Korea, Taiwan
Shade preference: Dappled to dense
USDA Zone: Z5
Description: A useful and vigorous plant for clothing a shady wall, its appeal lies in its self-clinging habit, the fresh green leaves and the heads of pretty white summer flowers. The only unfortunate characteristic is that it is deciduous, which means that the stems are bare in winter. But this does allow for us to see first hand the copper-coloured bark, and before the leaves drop they do turn to a magnificent golden yellow for a brief time.

ABOVE *Hydrangea petiolaris*

ABOVE *Lonicera periclymenum* 'Belgica'

Popular species and varieties: *H. petiolaris* is not the only climbing hydrangea, but is certainly the best known and easiest to obtain. It is also probably the hardiest. For the non-climbing, shrubby forms of *Hydrangea*, see page 142.

NAME: *LONICERA* (HONEYSUCKLE)

Origin: Europe, Asia
Shade preference: Dappled to light
USDA Zone: Z4–5
Description: The *Lonicera* genus is arguably the best known and loved of all scented climbers, and is certainly one of the best of the flowering climbers for shade. It is classed as a 'cottage garden plant', meaning that it is suited to older-style, rambling gardens where it can throw out its long shoots unhindered. Its scrambling habit is not neat enough to endure in today's smaller gardens, and it will not make a good subject for a piece of trelliswork on a house wall – it will just get too big with a mass of woody stems. The vigour of most types will envelop small buildings and sheds with relative ease.

Popular species and varieties: *Lonicera periclymenum* 'Belgica' in early summer produces loose, fragrant flower heads of purple and red-yellow; 'Serotina' AGM is purple and pink. *L. caprifolium* AGM carries yellow summer flowers; *L. japonica* 'Halliana' AGM is an evergreen form with fragrant summer flowers; *L. x brownii* 'Dropmore Scarlet' is not scented, but its rich red flowers last well into autumn.

ABOVE *Parthenocissus tricuspidata*

NAME: *PARTHENOCISSUS* (BOSTON IVY)

Origin: China, Japan, eastern US to Mexico
Shade preference: Dappled to dense
USDA Zone: Z3–7
Description: These creeping plants that will more or less completely cover a wall so that you cannot see the brickwork make such a spectacle in autumn, when the leaves turn red, that it can almost take your breath away. The common name of Virginia creepers often seems to be used for both *Parthenocissus tricuspidata* and *P. quinquefolia* AGM, although the former should really be called the Boston ivy. Its hand-like leaves are roughly similar to those of ivy, whereas the creeper's leaves are five-lobed and hence more delicate in appearance. On the whole, because of their deciduous nature these plants are not as good or as useful as ivy (which is evergreen), despite the fact that they are equally as tolerant of shade and poorish soil.
Popular species and varieties: *P. henryana* AGM has large bronze-green coloured leaves; *P. tricuspidata* 'Veitchii' is a superb form with small, three-lobed reddish-purple coloured leaves; *P. quinquefolia* AGM has leaves of five lobes, with similar colouring but is less dense.

NAME: *PASSIFLORA* (PASSIONFLOWER)

Origin: Brazil, Argentina, United States
Shade preference: Light
USDA Zone: Z7
Description: There are several kinds of passionflower, of varying degrees of hardiness. On a wall receiving sun for part of the day it should be possible to grow a lustrous plant of *Passiflora caerulea* AGM, probably the best-known form, with its distinctive blue fringe to the rather complex flower arrangement. The dark green lobed leaves are pleasant enough, but passionflowers are often shy to bloom, even in a sheltered spot.
Popular species and varieties: 'Constance Elliott' is an ivory white variety with yellow anthers. The maypop (*P. incarnata*) is the hardiest species, with somewhat smaller flowers yet still showy; it is actually a perennial climber, dying to the ground in winter but rapidly growing the following year to reach 20ft (6m) or so by late summer.

ABOVE *Passiflora caerulea* AGM

NAME: *TROPAEOLUM* (FLAME FLOWER)

Origin: Chile
Shade preference: Dappled
USDA Zone: Z8
Description: Another perennial climber (dying down at the end of each growing year, to re-emerge again the following year), there are few climbing plants with flowers as bright, and as vivid and as intense as this *Tropaeolum*. Closely related to the common annual nasturtium that grows in containers for summer colour, this is perhaps seen at its best when growing through and over shrubs, trees and hedging. Vibrant scarlet flowers are carried from mid-summer to mid-autumn. Once it is established, it will flower well, but it can sometimes take two or three years to build up a good root system before the flowers become a real spectacle.
Popular species and varieties: *Tropaeolum speciosum* AGM is the only species of note for a shady situation. There are no named forms.

ABOVE *Tropaeolum speciosum* AGM

TREES, SHRUBS AND CONIFERS

Most of the woody plants discussed in this section are garden shrubs rather than trees. By definition, trees are large subjects, usually with their heads in full sun. In fact, trees are very often the cause of the shade problem faced by other plants! I am including trees in the heading to this section, however, as many of the larger shrubs, such as box (*Buxus*) and yew (*Taxus*), are often thought of as small trees. Also, other types of shrub such as holly (*Ilex*) and *Pittosporum* can be grown large so that they develop into trees.

Included here as well are a few wall shrubs – these are not climbers, in that they do not have climbing mechanisms (such as twining shoots, tendrils and so on), but they do like to be grown on a wall for support. These include the silk tassel bush (*Garrya elliptica*).

Conifers are popular garden plants, especially since the 1970s when sales of them started to soar, and when breeding and development work intensified. Large conifers usually demand sunny conditions, but there are one or two forms that prefer shade.

NAME: *AUCUBA JAPONICA* 'VARIEGATA' (SPOTTED LAUREL)

Origin: China, Taiwan, Japan
Type: Evergreen shrub
Shade preference: Dappled to light
USDA Zone: Z7

Description: Thought of by many as 'boring', this is actually one of my favourite shrubs. It grows in the most shaded and difficult of places, beneath trees and in basement gardens. I was going to say that as long as they have a decent soil run they perform well, except I have

ABOVE *Aucuba japonica* 'Variegata'

just realized that I also have one growing in a container and it gets hardly any mollycoddling (just water in the summer). And the plant is a fine specimen. The richly-coloured, rounded evergreen leaves, with their cream and yellow spots, really shine in a shady nook – and it will even produce red berries if there are several plants growing nearby.

Popular species and varieties: *A. japonica* 'Crotonifolia' AGM has a larger proportion of yellow in the leaves, and also produces berries; *A. japonica* 'Picturata' has points to the leaves.

NAME: *BERBERIS* (BARBERRY)

Origin: Temperate parts worldwide
Type: Deciduous and evergreen shrubs
Shade preference: Dappled to light
USDA Zone: Z3–8
Description: The *Berberis* genus is huge, all characterized by the masses of yellow, orange or red flowers that appear, mainly, during early spring. There are deciduous types, but these mostly need full sun; it is the evergreen species that are happiest in dappled to light shade. Even better, these are undemanding shrubs – easy to grow and with no major pest and disease problems. The only word of warning is to watch out for the often vicious thorns on them (which does make them ideal as barrier or hedging plants, of course).

Popular species and varieties: *B. darwinii* AGM is, arguably, the best of them all; vivid orange flowers appear in late winter and spring, accompanied by the small, neat glossy evergreen leaves. *B. linearifolia* 'Orange King' is a deeper orange; *B. x stenophylla* 'Claret Cascade' is red-orange, whilst 'Corallina Compacta' AGM is coral pink. Then there is *B. thunbergii* AGM: this is a deciduous form, but is tolerant of dappled shade. It has many varieties, all of which are good, with flowers of pink, red or white but the reddish foliage, which turns fiery in autumn, is the main attraction.

ABOVE *Berberis darwinii* AGM

135

ABOVE *Buxus sempervirens* AGM

NAME: *BUXUS SEMPERVIRENS* AGM (BOX)

Origin: Southern Europe, Western Asia, North Africa

Type: Evergreen shrub to small tree

Shade preference: Dappled to dense

USDA Zone: Z5

Description: I just love box! It is nothing special to look at… just masses of small, leathery green leaves. In some forms the evergreen leaves are rounded, and in others they have a distinct point, especially when young. The flowers are hardly worth mentioning; in fact you would need to search hard to find them. However, *Buxus* makes very dense growth, meaning that it is perfect for training into topiary shapes, or hedging. It is incredibly shade-tolerant, and even on its own as a specimen shrub in a lawn it will look elegant. But for me, the gentlest of aromas produced when the leaves are lightly brushed up against is enough to send me into paroxysms of delight, for it reminds me of the box trees either side of my grandfather's front door when I was a child, long since gone. Some scents are most evocative.

Popular species and varieties: The straight species (*B. sempervirens* AGM) is usually found, and is very good. There are dozens of cultivated and specially bred varieties, and they are mostly very good, with some fine variegated forms, particularly *B. sempervirens* 'Elegantissima' AGM. Note, however, that planting variegated forms in shade will not produce the best colourings, for this they will need full sun.

NAME: *CAMELLIA*

Origin: Northern India, Himalayas, Japan, northern Indonesia

Type: Evergreen shrubs

Shade preference: Dappled to light

USDA Zone: Z8

Description: Along with rhododendrons and azaleas and *Pieris*, the *Camellia* is the other must-have flowering woodland shrub, especially if your soil is more acidic in nature (if your soil is chalky, you will need to grow all of these plants in specially constructed acid 'beds' or containers filled with acidic compost). Camellias are exquisite, with flowers in every shade of white, cream, pink or red. They do not perform well in full sun, preferring instead the dappled to light conditions of a woodland glade. But, equally important, these shrubs need to be sheltered from cold winds – this is often the reason for the buds falling before the flowers open, ruining what promises to be a healthy crop of spring flowers. The other rule with camellias is that they should not be planted where the buds and flowers receive early morning sun, as the quick thawing after a frost can weaken the flower cells, again making the buds and blooms fall. Late morning and afternoon sun, in small or dappled doses, is fine.

Popular species and varieties: There are hundreds to choose from, but here is a small selection that have performed very well for me: *C. japonica* 'Adolphe Audusson' AGM (deep red, semi-double), 'Alba Plena' (large double flowers of pure white); 'Elegans' AGM (peach pink), and 'Masayoshi' AGM sometimes known as 'Donckelaeri' (soft red, large and double). C. x williamsii 'Anticipation' AGM (deep pink), 'Donation' (deep pink, semi-double – the best-known Camellia of all), 'Contribution' (soft rose pink), 'Debbie' (large flowers of clear pink) and 'Les Jury' AGM (double, red flowers). Other hybrids worth looking for are 'Leonard Messel' AGM (peach pink), 'Inspiration' AGM (rich pink) and 'Cornish Snow' (white, single and small).

NAME: *CORNUS* (DOGWOOD)

Origin: Eastern North America
Type: Deciduous shrubs
Shade preference: Dappled to light
USDA Zone: Z2
Description: Cornus is a huge genus of shrubs and small trees, but most need full sun in order to thrive. The winter stem types (*C. sericea* and *C. alba*) both grow in the shade, but really need the winter sun to fall upon them in order to show off the brilliance of the stem colours.

Popular species and varieties: *C. sericea* 'Flaviramea' AGM is the best-known form, its yellow-green shoots combine well with the red-stemmed varieties, such as 'Cardinal' (scarlet shoots tipped orange). 'Budd's Yellow' has bright yellow young shoots. *C. alba* is the original red-barked dogwood, and many fine varieties of it have been bred: two of the best are 'Sibirica' AGM which is less robust, but it displays brilliant crimson-red winter stems; and 'Kesselringii' has unusual black-purple stems.

The creeping dogwood (*C. canadensis*) is a soil-hugging relative. This is one of the finest ground-covering plants for any shade garden; in mild areas it will remain evergreen. Delightful flowers appear in summer, each one having four striking white bracts accompanying the apple-green leaves.

ABOVE *Camellia x williamsii* 'Contribution'

ABOVE *Cornus sericea* 'Flaviramea' AGM

137

ABOVE *Corylopsis sinensis* var. *sinensis*

NAME: *CORYLOPSIS* (WINTER HAZEL)

Origin: China
Type: Deciduous shrubs
Shade preference: Dappled to light
USDA Zone: Z6
Description: These are delightful, underrated shrubs that should be grown much more often. Although they have 'hazel' in the common name, they are not related to the hazelnut, but are related to the witch hazel (*Hamamelis*) and share the appealing late-winter flowering habit. The flowers are yellow, pendent and delicately scented. You will need an acid soil to grow these plants to perfection.
Popular species and varieties: *C. pauciflora* AGM is the most often seen species, with flowers in groups of three. *C. sinensis* var. *sinensis* AGM has yellow-green flowers, and 'Spring Purple' has striking purple stems that contrast well with the leaves and flowers.

NAME: *COTONEASTER*

Origin: China
Type: Deciduous and evergreen shrubs
Shade preference: Dappled to light
USDA Zone: Z6
Description: There are a great many types of *Cotoneaster*, both evergreen and deciduous, ranging from mat-forming types that are good for ground cover, to medium and large shrubs and even tree-like forms. Most need a sunny spot to thrive in, but there are a few that prefer the dappled or lightly shaded spots in a garden.
Popular species and varieties: The following are all recommended for shade: *C. horizontalis* AGM, the herringbone cotoneaster, with small leaves, red berries and tinted leaves in autumn; *C. lacteus* AGM, small red berries that last well into winter; C. 'Rothschildianus', long green leaves and pale lemon-yellow berries in autumn; *C. salicifolius* 'Floccosus', similar leaves with red berries that last well into winter; and *C. simonsii*, which has white spring flowers, red autumn berries and makes a fine informal hedge.

ABOVE *Cotoneaster lacteus* AGM

NAME: *DAPHNE*

Origin: Europe, North Africa, temperate Asia
Type: Deciduous and evergreen shrubs
Shade preference: Dappled to light
USDA Zone: Z4–8
Description: Woodland daphnes are agreeable enough to look at: there is certainly no perception of ugliness surrounding them. But their appearance is not my reason for growing them. It is their scent, wafting across the garden on a still winter's day, that is like no other. The thick matt green leaves and the small whitish or pink flowers, and often the red berries as well are all attractive enough, but the fragrance will blow your socks off, and renders the *Daphne* essential planting near to a back door where, even during winter when occasional forays have to be made into the garden, it will be appreciated by all who walk past it.
Popular species and varieties: *D. odora* is a small, rounded, evergreen shrub with glossy, dark green leaves. Slightly hardier and more widely grown is *D. odora* 'Aureomarginata'

ABOVE *Daphne odora*

AGM, with narrow, cream-yellow margins around the leaves. The star-shaped mauve-purple flowers, carried in clusters, are wonderfully fragrant. *D. mezereum* is a deciduous, small shrub with upright branches. Purple-red flowers are carried in mid-winter on the previous year's shoots; red berries follow. *D. bholua* is a larger species, the best form being 'Jacqueline Postill' AGM, with highly scented blooms of purple-pink.

ABOVE *Fatsia japonica*

NAME: *FATSIA* (FALSE CASTOR OIL PLANT)

Origin: Japan
Type: Evergreen shrubs
Shade preference: Dappled to dense
USDA Zone: Z8

Description: This is the ultimate big, glossy evergreen plant – it has exotic-looking leaves and yet is hardy. A native of Japan, it grows well in any well-drained soil and tolerates any aspect. It is best in dappled or light shade, but I have also seen good examples of it in deep shade. When planted in full sun the palmate (hand-like) leaves turn more yellow in colour; in shade they are a rich, deep green. The flowers are creamy-white, and like giant ivy flowers, coming from the ends of the stems. *Fatsia* is also a good plant for a patio container, and grows well in coastal gardens, as it is conveniently tolerant of the salty air.

Popular species and varieties: The variegated form (*F. japonica* 'Variegata' AGM) is rather less vigorous than the plain form, and so is better if space is tight. The variegation is subtle: the grey-green leaves are tipped cream-white. Closely related is the hybrid it shares with the true ivy, x *Fatshedera lizei*: this is a tough character, tolerating heavy shade, coastal and polluted air. Although widely grown as a house plant, it is remarkably hardy and grows as a sprawling shrub, providing excellent ground cover. x *Fatshedera lizei* 'Variegata' AGM has irregular white margins to its grey-green leaves.

NAME: *FUCHSIA* (HARDY FUCHSIA)

Origin: South America, East Africa, Hawaii, New Zealand, Ireland
Type: Deciduous shrubs
Shade preference: Dappled to light
USDA Zone: Z6

Description: The *Fuchsia* is usually associated with the summer-flowering pot and container (and sometimes bedding) plants, and these are tender. They are sun-lovers generally, sometimes thriving in dappled shade. The hardy fuchsias, however, are much more shade tolerant. Although they are called 'hardy' they really only do well in milder locations, and a really severe winter will cause them serious damage. These hardier types also flower for longer, from early summer until late autumn; I regularly have flowers on my plants in early winter when a night frost can give a coating to the last remaining of them.

Popular species and varieties: The best-known hardy fuchsia is *F. magellanica* var. *gracilis* AGM, a very graceful and pretty shrub, with slender, arching stems and numerous small, delicate flowers of scarlet and purple. 'Mrs Popple' AGM has large flowers of scarlet and violet and a compact habit; 'Riccartonii' AGM is probably the best *Fuchsia* for general planting where a tall shrub can be accommodated. 'Tom Thumb' AGM is a dwarf shrub, with masses of small, freely produced blooms of scarlet and violet. 'Lady Thumb' AGM is similar in habit, with red and white flowers. Larger, but also with red and white flowers, is 'Snowcap' AGM.

ABOVE *Fuchsia magellanica* var. *gracilis* AGM

ABOVE *Garrya elliptica*

NAME: *GARRYA ELLIPTICA* (SILK TASSEL BUSH)

Origin: Western US
Type: Evergreen shrub, preferably by a wall
Shade preference: Dappled to light
USDA Zone: Z8
Description: Growing to around 10ft (3m) in height, this shrub really deserves to be planted next to a wall, where it will get protection from cold winds. For this reason it is one of those shrubs classed as 'wall plants' without actually being a climber. Its best feature is the mass of winter catkins it produces, grey-green at first, then becoming a dull cream. It has thick, leathery green leaves.
Popular species and varieties: Only the species *Garrya elliptica* is in general cultivation; 'James Roof' AGM is the best variety, with thicker and longer catkins, some 14in (35cm) long.

NAME: *HYDRANGEA*

Origin: China, Japan, Indonesia, Philippines, North and South America
Type: Woodland shrubs
Shade preference: Dappled to light
USDA Zone: Z3–9
Description: Hydrangeas are a feature of the summer garden, the most familiar being the pink or blue 'mophead' and white or green 'lacecap' hydrangeas. Few gardeners, however, appreciate the whole scope of this genus, which includes a great many species and cultivars, many with white flowers; (the climbing hydrangea, *H. petiolaris*, is discussed on page 130). Most are good plants for the dappled light at the edge of a woodland garden. Strangely, hydrangeas seem to look incongruous in the harsh, even shade cast by buildings.
Popular species and varieties: *Hydrangea paniculata* 'Grandiflora' AGM is one of the most breathtaking and showy of large shrubs. It cannot fail to grab attention as it erupts from the back of the border, with its large conical flowerheads resembling huge lilac blossoms. The flowers start to appear pale green in summer, then turn slowly through cream to creamy white with flushes of pink. In shade the cream colour is more pure.

The oak-leaved hydrangea (*H. quercifolia* AGM) is one of the most underrated of all shrubs. Of medium size, it is an architectural plant with its bold lobed leaves that resemble those of oak – but are much bigger. They also produce fine autumn colours. Conical, white flowerheads appear in late summer. In the variety 'Snow Queen' they are larger still.

H. macrophylla (the mophead hydrangea) has numberous varieties, and among the best are 'Ami Pasquier' AGM (red on a chalky soil, purple on acid) and 'Blauer Prinz' (pink on chalk and blue on acid). *H. aspera* Villosa Group AGM is a pink-lilac lace-cap type.

ABOVE *Hydrangea quercifolia* 'Snow Queen'

NAME: *HYPERICUM CALYCINUM* (ST JOHN'S WORT)

Origin: South-eastern Europe
Type: Evergreen shrub
Shade preference: Dappled to dense
USDA Zone: Z6
Description: With its five-petalled flowers of golden yellow, and prominent stamens, this *Hypericum* (also known as the rose of Sharon) is an easy-to-grow, undemanding shrub. It can be relied upon to brighten up even the dullest parts of the garden. It is good under trees or on dry banks. It is a thug, however, and can spread beyond its allocated patch.
Popular species and varieties: Although there are many forms of *Hypericum*, apart from *H. calycinum* they are nearly always better in full sun.

ABOVE *Hypericum calycinum*

143

ABOVE *Ilex x altaclarensis* 'Golden King'

NAME: *ILEX* (HOLLY)

Origin: Europe, Africa, Asia
Type: Evergreen shrubs or small trees
Shade preference: Light
USDA Zone: Z5–6
Description: Who can think of holly without thinking of prickly leaves and of Christmas decorations? This large group of shrubs has much to offer, with leaves of all shapes and sizes, all shades of green and many with variegations. Many varieties have red berries, whilst others have yellow or black (and there is supposed even to be a fabled white-berried holly, but nobody has one in cultivation). There are a few deciduous forms, but most are evergreen. There are even types with rounded, prickle-less leaves. Hollies, it has to be said, are grown for their leaves and berries; the flowers are utterly insignificant. Berries are carried on female forms, so it is important that a male plant is nearby in order to cross-pollinate. Take time to look up a variety before buying, as names can be misleading (see 'Golden King' below). The variegated forms are really at their best in full sun, where the leaf colourings can be seen at their best; the all-green forms, however, are fine for light shade.

Popular species and varieties: The common holly (*I. aquifolium* AGM) has numerous hybrids and cultivars, and these can vary enormously in size, habit and colourings. The species itself has dark green leaves and red berries. 'Bacciflava' has yellow berries; 'J.C. van Tol' AGM has narrow leaves with few spines and red berries; 'Golden Queen' AGM (a male form, curiously) has no berries but dark leaves with gold edges; and 'Pyramidalis Fructo Luteo' AGM has dark green leaves and yellow berries. *I. x altaclarensis* 'Cameliifolia' AGM has few spines, large glossy leaves, purple shoots and red berries. 'Golden King' (a female form) has variegated leaves and red berries; *I. pernyi* is different, with small, oblong, dark green spiny leaves, with red autumn berries.

NAME: *MAHONIA* (OREGON GRAPE)

Origin: Asia, North and Central America
Type: Evergreen shrubs
Shade preference: Dappled to dense
USDA Zone: Z5–9
Description: Mahonias have long been some of our most popular winter-flowering evergreens. With their stiff stems and strange leaf arrangement, they are awkward as young plants

144

ABOVE *Mahonia aquifolium*

but acquire grace with maturity. Their leathery texture belies their delicate beauty and the soft fragrance of the flowers, carried on long, spreading racemes.

Popular species and varieties: *M. japonica* AGM is the best-known species. Although it grows on virtually any soil, if grown on poor, shallow soils some leaves display rich scarlet and red shades that last well into the winter. It is one of the most fragrant of mahonias; in mid-winter delightful soft primrose yellow flowers come from the terminal rosettes of leaves. *M. aquifolium* produces bright yellow flowers in rather dense clusters. The best of the hybrids, less hardy than most but stronger in flower, is *M. x media* 'Charity'. *M. wagneri* 'Undulata' has wavy leaves, but is less tolerant of poor soil.

NAME: *PHILADELPHUS* (MOCK ORANGE)

Origin: Central and North America, Eastern Asia
Type: Deciduous shrubs
Shade preference: Dappled to light
USDA Zone: Z5–9
Description: These tallish shrubs are well known for their early summer scented white flowers. But they are not really thought to have any other

particular virtue. However, their tolerance to shade is one that should be appreciated more. All are deciduous.

Popular species and varieties: Perhaps the best for a shady spot is *P. coronarius* 'Aureus' AGM: it is more compact than most, and has golden-yellow leaves in spring and early summer. As they age, the leaves turn to light green. In shade, the foliage does not burn like it can in full sun, and its brightness can really transform a dull corner. Clusters of small white flowers appear, but they are not particularly showy against the foliage. *P.* 'Belle Etoile' AGM produces masses of white flowers, each with golden stamens, in mid-summer. It will be shy to flower, however, in the deepest shade, but in dappled shade it will thrive.

ABOVE *Philadelphus* 'Belle Etoile' AGM

ABOVE *Pieris formosa* var. *forrestii*

NAME: *PIERIS* (FOREST FLAME)

Origin: Japan, China, Taiwan, Vietnam, Himalayas, Nepal
Type: Evergreen woodland shrubs, sometimes large and almost tree-like
Shade preference: Dappled to light
USDA Zone: Z5–7
Description: These shrubs really are at their best in spring, when their displays of white, bell-shaped lily-of-the-valley like blossoms appear, closely followed by the new season's young shoots in fiery reds or delicate pinks and creams. The unfortunate thing is that this new

growth is usually produced before the risk of frost has passed, and they are easily scorched by it. As a member of the heather and *Rhododendron* family, *Pieris* needs an acid soil.
Popular species and varieties: *P. formosa* var. *forrestii* has superbly vivid red and cream young shoots in spring; *P.* 'Forest Flame' AGM (not to be confused with the common name for the genus) produces young leaves that are rather more red; *P. floribunda* is one of the hardiest, and one of the best for flowers; and *P. japonica* 'Purity' AGM has very long flower racemes.

NAME: *RHODODENDRON*

Origin: Worldwide, mainly the temperate regions of Asia
Type: Deciduous and evergreen small shrubs to medium-sized, spreading trees
Shade preference: Light to dense
USDA Zone: Z5–9
Description: Well known and much loved by gardeners, these are some of the most spectacular of all flowering plants. The *Rhododendron* genus is enormous, most of which are grown for their flower colours in everything from rich vibrant shades to more subtle and pastel colours. Azaleas are just one of the smaller-forms of *Rhododendron*, and these usually have the strongest-coloured flowers. Most bloom in spring, although some offer up their colour in mid-winter, whilst others (such as the white-flowering 'Polar Bear') bloom well into summer. A wide variation also is to be had with the foliage; some forms have leaves barely $\frac{3}{4}$in (1.5cm) across, whilst others are the size of oval dinner plates. This is a genus of woodland plants, so conditions from dappled to dense shade will suit different types. The tougher forms will survive happily in full sun, but even these are likely to perform better still in some shade. They are lime haters, so require acidic soil. If you have chalky soil, you will either need to create a special bed with imported acid soil, or grow them in containers with ericaceous compost.

ABOVE *Rhododendron* 'Loderi Group'

Popular species and varieties: It is difficult to select and describe just a handful of these shrubs, when so many are available, but the following are large-flowered hybrids I have had personal experience of growing. Among those with yellow blooms are 'Julie' (pale lemon), 'Hotei' AGM (deep yellow) and 'Queen Elizabeth II' AGM (greenish yellow). For pink flowers there is 'Augfast Group', 'Loderi Group' and 'Percy Wiseman' AGM (all blush pink) and 'Morgenrot' (deep rose pink, almost red). 'Britannia' and 'Baden-Baden' (both red) are old favourites, and then there is 'Dopey' AGM (bright orange-red). A good white form, 'Helene Schiffner' AGM, has buds that start off mauve, opening to pure white. Similarly the old variety 'Sappho' is excellent, with buds that start off mauve and open to white, but each of the white blooms has a central deep purple blotch.

'Sapphire' is, I believe, the best of the blues, and even this in some lights looks more like lilac.

The deciduous hybrid azaleas are usually smaller, and prefer being sited in light shade rather than dappled shade. Look for 'Glowing Embers' (orange-red) and 'Gibraltar' AGM (flame orange). With a name like 'Satan' AGM, a plant could only be red, and this is an intense geranium-red. 'Persil' AGM has masses of white blooms with orange-yellow markings.

Smaller still are the evergreen hybrid group referred to as Japanese azaleas. In some years they just about cover themselves with flower so that you cannot see any leaves. Look for 'Palestrina' AGM (white), 'Mother's Day' AGM (rose red), 'Vuyk's Scarlet' AGM (bright red), 'Hinomayo' AGM (clear pink) and 'Hatsugiri' (magenta-purple).

147

ABOVE *Rubus thibetanus* AGM

NAME: *RUBUS* (ORNAMENTAL BRAMBLE)

Origin: China
Type: Cane shrubs
Shade preference: Dappled to light
USDA Zone: Z6
Description: Wild brambles are the scourge of many gardens, but there are some very fine ornamental brambles that deserve to be planted. There is a certain irony that the wild, weed bramble will frequent dry, shady places under large trees. These weeds should be removed, and the space made available is then perfect for their more decorative cousins.

Popular species and varieties: *R. cockburnianus* (white, thorny stems) and *R. thibetanus* AGM (brown canes with a white covering) are both dramatic plants for the winter garden, after leaf-fall so that the stems can be seen to best advantage. They will grow in shade, but deserve a sunny spot, which will better show off the stems. Particularly useful is the ground-covering *R. tricolor* with reddish stems and mid-green, bristly leaves; this relative, however, does not mind dense shade.

NAME: *RUSCUS ACULEATUS* (BUTCHER'S BROOM)

Origin: Europe
Type: Evergreen shrub
Shade preference: Dappled to dense
USDA Zone: Z7
Description: This is, quite honestly, more of a 'curio' than a valuable garden plant. It is a talking point and is, I suppose, more of a plant for a plant-collector rather than a gardener. It is evergreen, but what appear to be the leaves are actually flatted stems, the true leaves being scale-like and so tiny as to go unnoticed for most of the time. Red berries appear on female plants, but only if males are grown nearby. The main benefit of this plant, apart from its botanical uniqueness, is that it will grow in deep, dry, shady places where little else will.
Popular species and varieties: *R. aculeatus* is the main species available; it is a matter of luck as to whether you buy a male or female.

NAME: *SKIMMIA*

Origin: Eastern Asia
Type: Evergreen shrubs
Shade preference: Dappled to light
USDA Zone: Z7
Description: Popular in landscaping and gardens, so often these plants are grown in full sun, where the leaves become olive-yellow, making the plant look unhealthy. In shade, however, the leaves remain rich green, and if

ABOVE *Ruscus aculeatus*

the soil is moist and acidic, so much the better. Skimmias generally produce small, insignificant flowers, so apart from the evergreen foliage it is the berries for which these plants are grown mainly. Both male and female plants will need to be grown in close proximity in order to get the bright red berries.

Popular species and varieties: *S. japonica* has bright orange red berries whereas the cultivar 'Wakehurst White' has white berries, and 'Nymans' AGM has bright red berries. 'Rubella' AGM is a male form, therefore does not produce berries, however its main attraction comes in the form of its large clusters of many tiny red flower buds. *S. x confusa* 'Kew Green' AGM does have small, white flowers that are delicately fragrant.

ABOVE *Skimmia x confusa* 'Kew Green' AGM

ABOVE *Taxus baccata*

NAME: *TAXUS* (YEW)

Origin: Europe and Western Asia
Type: Evergreen conifer; shrub, tree or trained as a hedge
Shade preference: Dappled to light
USDA Zone: Z6
Description: There are few shade-loving conifers, but the yew is one of them. It will tolerate dry soil, and as it is not averse to tight clipping, is one of the few plants that can be grown into a hedge in the shade of a large tree. All parts of the yew are poisonous, and young children should always be kept away from the tempting wax-like berries.
Popular species and varieties: For hedging, always go for the straight *Taxus baccata*, with mid- to deep green foliage and bright red berries. 'Fastigiata' is an upright-growing form which is best seen as a specimen plant on its own. 'Fastigiata Aurea' and 'Fastigiata Aureomarginata' are upright-growing, golden and variegated versions.

NAME: *VIBURNUM*

Origin: Temperate northern hemisphere, extending into South America and Malaysia
Type: Deciduous and evergreen shrubs
Shade preference: Dappled to light
USDA Zone: Z2–9
Description: This is a very large genus of shrubs, with some 150 species and many cultivars. It is a hugely versatile genus, and most forms are undemanding and easy to grow. Many are noted for their wonderful fragrances – particularly the winter-flowering types.
Popular species and varieties: Probably the best known is the evergreen *V. tinus* and its cultivars, individual plants of which can flower intermittently for eight or nine months of the year. Flowers are generally white with the merest hint of pink. 'Eve Price' is more compact growing and 'Gwenllian' has more pink in the bloom. The deciduous *V. x bodnantense* produces clusters of sweet-smelling pink flowers on its bare branches throughout winter, starting often as

early as mid-autumn; 'Dawn' is my favourite of the cultivars available – its rose-pink blooms slowly darkening as they age. *V. davidii* AGM is a low-growing evergreen with large, oval, glossy dark green leaves with characteristic linear grooves. Long-lasting berries of bright blue, on reddish stalks, follow the small early summer flowers. *V. carlesii* produces vibrant white flowers in spring and early summer.

NAME: *VINCA* (PERIWINKLE)

Origin: Northern Asia, Europe
Type: Low, ground-covering shrub
Shade preference: Dappled to dense
USDA Zone: Z4–9
Description: Vincas are good trailing, ground cover plants with prostrate or arching shoots. In the landscape they are most effective when covering a bank, and they'll readily colonize dry, shady places under trees. The common name of periwinkle comes from the Middle English *per wynke*, referring to wreath making. This is because the long, flexible stems of *Vinca* are suitable for winding around, and binding, curved frames.

Popular species and varieties: *V. major* is the large or greater periwinkle. It's a shrubby, carpeting or trailing shrub that has good shade tolerance and provides excellent dense cover except on very dry, or exposed sites, or on poorly drained soils. It is vigorous, however. Its star-shaped flowers are blue or white and appear in spring. *V. major* 'Variegata' has leaves with pale green blotches and margins of cream-yellow; the flowers are in shades of violet. One of its parents is *V. major* var. *oxyloba*, which is very vigorous, forming a dense rampant cover. *V. minor* is the dwarf or lesser periwinkle. It is a smaller-leaved species, but nevertheless offers very effective ground cover in similar conditions. It also tolerates both deep shade and full sun.

ABOVE **Viburnum tinus**

ABOVE **Vinca major**

VEGETABLES AND FRUITING PLANTS

It's not often that you will find any reference to vegetables and fruiting plants in a book about gardening in the shade. This is because nearly all edible plants require copious quantities of sunshine in which to form, develop and ripen. There are more vegetables to grow in shade than fruits, but this is not really saying much, as together they represent just a handful of types. Listed in the panel (on page 155) are the fruits that can be grown in gardens that receive a little shade for part of the day. These are quite specific, as sun is needed to ripen fruit. It is not as appropriate, therefore, to list vegetables in this way. If you fancy growing some vegetables in an area that gets shade for some of the time, it is certainly worth a try. Detailed below are the seven crops that I have had success with in dappled and light shade. I do urge you to try growing your own produce even if your garden has copious shade as we all know how important fresh fruit and vegetables are.

ABOVE **Jerusalem artichoke (tubers)**

NAME: ARTICHOKE, JERUSALEM (*HELIANTHUS TUBEROSUS*)

Origin: Canada, south-eastern US
Type: Hardy perennial
Shade preference: Dappled to light
USDA Zone: Z4
Description: Grown for their edible knobbly tubers, the above-ground parts can reach 10ft (3m) or more, so you will need to give this plant some space in which to grow. They are undoubtedly at their best in full sun, but will tolerate and perform well in dappled light and half shade.
Popular species and varieties: 'Fuseau' has a smoothish skin; 'Boston Red' has a rose-red skin and is a particularly knobbly variety

NAME: BLUEBERRIES, HIGHBUSH (*VACCINIUM CORYMBOSUM*)

Origin: Eastern US
Type: Fruiting shrub
Shade preference: Dappled to light
USDA Zone: Z6–8
Description: There are 'highbush' and 'lowbush' blueberries; the former tolerate some shade (but prefer full sun), whilst the latter need sun. Being members of the heather and *Rhododendron* family, these plants need an acid soil, and they also like a cool, moist climate. The purple-black fruits, covered in a grey 'bloom' are delicious in cooked desserts; they need to be really ripe to be enjoyed raw. These plants also have ornamental value, as the leaves turn to brilliant yellows and golds in summer.
Popular species and varieties: 'Berkeley' is the best-known variety; it is a mid-season crop. 'Jersey' is a compact late-season variety.

ABOVE **Blueberry 'Berkeley'**

NAME: CORN SALAD (*VALERIANELLA LOCUSTA*)

Origin: Europe
Type: Hardy annual
Shade preference: Dappled to light
USDA Zone: Z2
Description: Also known as lamb's lettuce, this can be cropped all year round. Used as a substitute for lettuce, the leaves are shiny, dark green and with a delicate flavour. With a winter crop, do not remove more than a few leaves at a time, or you will seriously deplete the plant.
Popular species and varieties: 'Large Leaved' is a good winter variety; 'Jade' has particularly tender and delicious leaves.

ABOVE **Corn salad**

ABOVE **Rhubarb 'Timperley Early'**

NAME: RHUBARB (*RHEUM x CULTORUM*)

Origin: Garden hybrids, with the original forms of *Rheum* originating in China and Tibet
Type: Hardy perennial
Shade preference: Dappled
USDA Zone: Z2–5
Description: All of the gardening books I've ever seen maintain that rhubarb needs a position in full sun. It certainly likes the sun, but I have grown some very healthy crops of rhubarb in distinctly dappled conditions, under a large pear tree at the far end of the kitchen garden. Not knowing what else to plant there I tried the rhubarb, and it has performed magnificently over the years.
Popular species and varieties: 'Champagne' is a good old variety, fast-growing with green stalks tinged red; 'Timperley Early' has thin, succulent stalks, good for forcing.

NAME: ROCKET (*ERUCA VESICARIA*)

Origin: Mediterranean
Type: Hardy annual
Shade preference: Dappled to light
USDA Zone: Z7
Description: Having a delicious, tangy, peppery taste without being bitter, this salad leaf vegetable is hardy and vigorous, and will thrive on most soils. It prefers full sun, but gives a good account of itself in dappled and light shade
Popular species and varieties: Only the straight species is grown.

NAME: SPINACH (*SPINACIA OLERACEA*)

Origin: South-west Asia
Type: Hardy annual
Shade preference: Dappled to light
USDA Zone: Z5
Description: Spinach prefers an open site, but can cope extremely well in dappled or light shade. It is a fast-growing crop, so you can

ASPECTS FOR GROWING FRUIT

All fruits enjoy a sunny aspect, but what about gardens that face one of the three directions that gets less direct sunshine?

◆ West-facing gardens, which get afternoon sun, are suitable for growing apples, apricots, blackberries, cherries, currants (red and white, not black), gages, gooseberries, grapes, nectarines, peaches and raspberries.

◆ An east-facing garden is more difficult, as it is usually colder; the sun shines on it in the early morning, and then moves away before it has the chance to warm up properly. Fruits that can succeed here include apples, blackberries, cherries, currants (all types), gooseberries, plums, early pears and raspberries.

◆ In gardens with the coldest aspect, where the sun is behind the house for most of the day, you could try the following: culinary apples, blackberries, currants, damsons and gooseberries.

ABOVE **Spinach 'Triton'**

have several harvests from it in the one growing season. However, in hot, intensely sunny weather, or if the soil dries out, spinach will quickly 'bolt', and spinach generally is susceptible to downy mildew fungal disease. Individual leaves should be picked regularly, to encourage resprouting; this also helps to improve air circulation around the plants, helping to prevent mildew.

Popular species and varieties: 'Bloomsdale' has delicious, dark green leaves; 'Matador' has larger leaves of mid-green; 'Triton' tastes good and is particularly resistant to mildew.

NAME: WATERCRESS (*RORIPPA NASTURTIUM-AQUATICUM*)

Origin: Europe, south-west Asia,
Type: Hardy aquatic perennial
Shade preference: Dappled to light
USDA Zone: Z6
Description: The leaves are said to be tangy, peppery, spicy... whatever your perception, there is nothing to beat them as a filling in an egg sandwich! Watercress grows naturally in freshwater streams, so is not easy to grow in a small garden; you will need to start by creating a watercourse. Although moving water in which to grow is not a pre-requisite of this plant, this is where it is happiest. You can get away with growing it in very moist soil, but then it will be essential to have light shade so that the ground does not become dry in summer.

Popular species and varieties: Only the straight species is grown.

Glossary

Acid
With a pH value below 7; acid soil is deficient in lime and basic minerals.

Alkaline
With a pH value above 7.

Annual
Plant grown from seed that germinates, flowers, sets seed and dies in one growing year.

Bare-root
Plants sold with their roots bare of soil (ie. not in a pot or container).

Biennial
A plant that grows from seed and completes its life cycle within two years.

Bolting
Premature flower and seed production.

Cultivar
A cultivated plant clearly distinguished by one or more characteristics and which retains these characteristics when propagated; a contraction of 'cultivated variety', and often abbreviated to 'cv.' in plant naming.

Deadheading
The removal of spent flowers or flowerheads.

Deciduous
Plant that loses its leaves at the end of every growing year, and which renews them at the start of the next.

Dieback
Death of shoots, starting from the tips, and as a result of damage or disease.

Double
Referred to in flower terms as a bloom with several layers of petals; usually there would be a minimum of 20 petals. 'Very double' flowers have more than 40 petals.

Genus (pl. Genera)
A category in plant naming, comprising a group of related species.

Ground cover
Usually low-growing plants that grow over the soil, so suppressing weed growth.

Hardwood cutting
Method of propagation by which a cutting is taken from mature wood at the end of the growing season.

Heeling in
Laying plants in the soil, with the roots covered, as a temporary measure until full planting can take place.

Hybrid
The offspring of genetically different parents, usually produced in cultivation, but occasionally arising in the wild.

Mulch
Layer of material applied to the soil surface, to conserve moisture, improve its structure, protect roots from frost and suppress weeds.

Perennial

Plant that lives for at least three seasons.

pH scale

A scale measured from 1–14 that indicates the alkalinity or acidity of soil. pH 7 is neutral; pH 1–7 is acid, pH 7–14 is alkaline.

Root-ball

The roots and surrounding soil or compost visible when a plant is removed from a pot.

Rootstock

A plant used to provide the root system for a grafted plant.

Sideshoot

A stem that arises from the side of a main shoot or stem.

Single

In flower terms, a single layer of petals opening out into a fairly flat shape, comprising no more than five petals.

Species

A category in plant naming, the rank below genus, containing related, individual plants.

Sucker

Generally a shoot that arises from below ground, emanating from a plant's roots, but also refers to any shoot on a grafted plant that originates from below the graft union.

Variety

Botanically, a naturally occurring variant of a wild species; usually shorted to 'var.' in plant naming.

About the author

Graham Clarke was born into gardening – literally. His father was in charge of the world-famous Regent's Park in London and at the time of Graham's birth the family lived in a lodge within the public gardens there. During his formative years Graham was surrounded by quality horticulture, so it was little surprise when he chose this as his career. He went to study with England's Royal Horticultural Society at Wisley Gardens, and after that worked as a gardener at Buckingham Palace in London. This very private garden is seen by Her Majesty the Queen on most of the days she is in residence.

For more than 20 years Graham has been a gardening writer and journalist. He has written eight books, and countless articles for most of the major UK gardening magazines. He has been the editor of *Amateur Gardening* (the UK's leading weekly magazine for amateurs) and *Horticulture Week* (the UK's leading weekly magazine for professionals), and is now a freelance garden writer and consultant. He lives in Dorset, on England's south coast, with his wife, two daughters and many shade-loving plants!

Index

Pages highlighted in **bold** indicate photographs of plants.

GMC Publications Ltd, 166 High Street, Lewes, East Sussex BN7 1XU, United Kingdom
Tel: 01273 488005 Fax: 01273 402866
www.gmcbooks.com

Contact us for a complete catalogue, or visit our website.